The Religious Significance

of Atheism

NUMBER 18
BAMPTON LECTURES
IN AMERICA
DELIVERED AT
COLUMBIA UNIVERSITY
1966

The Religious Significance

of Atheism

ALASDAIR MAC INTYRE

AND PAUL RICŒUR

Columbia University Press

New York

Alasdair MacIntyre is Professor of Sociology
at the University of Essex.

Paul Ricœur is Professor of Philosophy
at the Faculté des Lettres et Sciences Humaines
of Nanterre.

Copyright © 1969 Columbia University Press
SBN 0-231-03139-4
Library of Congress Catalog Card Number: 68-28398
Printed in the United States of America
10 9 8 7 6 5 4 3

Preface

THE PROBLEM
of contemporary atheism is discussed in these Bampton Lectures from two quite different standpoints. One of us has been concerned with the cultural significance of the debate about)belief in God and would argue that the religious significance of this debate can be understood only in a wider cultural context. The other has addressed himself more directly to the philosophical and theological issues. At the time at which we were preparing these lectures, neither of us had any indication of what the other was going to say. Thus our arguments are in no way coordinated and in no way designed to be directed against one another. But the very different perspectives in which we have viewed the central problems are obviously not irrelevant to each other. Contemporary atheism seen with MacIntyre's eyes is not quite the same as contemporary atheism seen with Ricœur's eyes; and the arguments of the two pairs of lectures raise a number of questions over and above those raised by the central theme itself. Perhaps the most important of these new questions concerns the whole relationship of sociological analysis to philosophical argument.

However we may disagree in other matters we agree in one thing, our gratitude to Columbia University not only for having invited us to give the lectures but for the warmth of its hospitality during the period in which we gave them.

ALASDAIR MAC INTYRE

PAUL RICŒUR

December 1, 1968

Contents

The Debate about God:
Victorian Relevance
and Contemporary Irrelevance

ALASDAIR MACINTYRE

The Fate of Theism

EVEN IN THE PRESENT DAY
many individuals undergo private, stylized versions of
that break with theistic, and especially Christian, beliefs
which was so marked a feature of Victorian culture. Because this is true of culture heroes of our time as various
as Bertrand Russell and Jean Paul Sartre, we may tend to
underrate the difference between the central part the experience of that break played in the culture of the nineteenth century and the peripheral part it plays in our
culture today. I suggest that the recent debate between
theists and atheists has been insufficiently self-conscious
for the most part, and that what is primarily important is
not so much to make fresh moves in this debate as to re-
consider just how crucial the debate actually is.

Mrs. Humphrey Ward's best-selling novel of 1888,
Robert Elsmere, which describes a transition from orthodox Christianity not to what we might think of as
pure atheism but to a set of undogmatic religious attitudes, is nevertheless a perceptive portrait of what those
who made the more radical break with theism characteristically underwent. For even a radical atheist such as

Ludwig Feuerbach, while concerned with refuting the formulations of the Christian religion, still wished to maintain its essence, once it had been detached from its supernatural trappings; and the philosophy of T. H. Green, which Robert Elsmere acquired in place of Christianity, is theistic only in a Pickwickian sense. The inclusion of the character and philosophy of T. H. Green in Mrs. Ward's novel is very important: if she was to be realistic in representing Robert Elsmere's loss of faith, she had to show his encounter with some of the central intellectual issues of his day. This encounter above all distinguishes the debate of the nineteenth century, not only from that of the twentieth but also from earlier debates. Hume could question theism on grounds that, original in detail though they are, had been available in kind for millennia; similarly Cardinal Newman could retort to him with arguments which, however imaginative they may be, could have been used without anachronism at any time before. But most of those whose belief was put in question in the mid-nineteenth century had to cope with issues unique to their culture: Darwinian biology; the philosophical theories derived from Hegel (whether by continental Feuerbachians or by Green and Bradley); and perhaps above all the new techniques of historical criticism, which both partly grew out of and found their most radical assumptions in the quest for the historical Jesus. Robert Elsmere, for example, finds himself inquiring why the assumpts of the new medieval history were not carried over to the study of the New Testament. If some defeat inflicted on the barbarians during their invasions of the Roman Empire is explained in a medieval document as due to a miraculous intervention, the rules of modern historical discipline do not permit a historian to entertain for a moment the possibility that this explanation is correct; why, Robert Elsmere argues, should the New Testament record be treated in any different way?

The manner in which the advancing applications of rational method lay directly athwart the theistic issue in the nineteenth century is not duplicated today. The science of cybernetics, the physics of fundamental particles, the problems of sociological theory, do not seem to raise with the same immediacy questions about religion. The tension of the choice between the beliefs of theism and the truths embedded in contemporary culture, a tension which was so real for men like Henry Sidgwick and Matthew Arnold, leaves no mark on intellectuals now.

At once it may be said that this comment may reflect upon the nature of contemporary culture, but not upon the issue that divides theism from atheism. That issue, the theist will claim, remains and must remain the same yesterday, today, and forever. (And that it certainly must so remain in the theist's perspective tells us something important about his perspective.) But in order to engage with this claim of the theist, I must ask whether what is at least a decline in the urgency of the debate and what may be, as I shall be claiming, a change in its whole character may not be connected with, indeed explained by, more fundamental changes in our culture.

One act which reveals our cultural perspective is our choice of calendar. Should we reckon the modern period

to have begun in the time of Christ, in the year of the
Hegira, or in the first year of the French Revolution? Or
perhaps the calendar of secularized man ought to be di-
vided into these two periods: the first from the New
Stone Age to the nineteenth century, the second there-
after. What breaks would this division signal? The origin
of the first period has been speculated upon by Claude
Lévi-Strauss. He argues that the technological revolution
of neolithic man must have been the outcome of a long
and brilliant study of nature. The medicines, food, and
metal-working of neolithic man all presuppose a system
of classification and theory by which nature was understood and could be subdued. Lévi-Strauss therefore argues that the reply to Lucien Lévy-Bruhl's characterization of the primitive mind as prelogical and irrational
should be not merely the weaker and commoner assertion that in his own times the primitive was rational
even though his system of thought differs profoundly
from modern science. Rather we should conclude that
the primitive is as scientific as we are:

. . . there are two distinct modes of scientific thought. These
are certainly not a function of different stages of development of the human mind but rather of two strategic levels
at which nature is accessible to scientific enquiry: one
roughly adapted to that of perception and the imagination:
the other at a remove from it. It is as if the necessary connections which are the object of all science, neolithic or
modern, could be arrived at by two different routes, one
very close to, and the other more remote from, [direct sense
experience]. [*The Savage Mind*, tr. from the French, *La*

Pensée sauvage (Chicago, University of Chicago Press, 1966), p. 15, writes "sensible intuition" for the last phrase.]

That Lévi-Strauss's marvelous ingenuity in mapping the logical patterns of primitive systems of classification is indeed the discovery of a whole mode of understanding nature I have no wish to deny; but that this mode can properly be called scientific in anything like the sense in which modern physics is so called seems to betray a misunderstanding at once of science and of the sharp contrast between scientific modes of thought and the primitive modes analyzed by Lévi-Strauss. We can begin to understand why this is so if we consider a second thesis advanced by Lévi-Strauss in *The Savage Mind* —namely, that how men conceive the relations between nature and culture is a function of the modification of their social relations, a thesis which leads Lévi-Strauss to see the closest logical and symbolic relationships between the concepts and categories by which primitive man understands his own society and those by which he understands nature. But this thesis at once undermines the characterization of primitive thought as scientific. For the relative unalterability of primitive social structure suggests that the conceptual schemes of primitive man are essentially inflexible. By contrast, modern science—although its modes of activity and its institutional bases may owe much to the form of the society in which they arose—is autonomous in its capacity for change independent of social change or social stability. Attempts to deny this by insisting that the Darwinian theory of natural selection mirrors the competitive struggles of

Victorian capitalism or that seventeenth-century mechanics reflects the contemporary preoccupations of the bourgeoisie at best merely draw our attention to certain coincidental analogies. Such analogies miss the major point, however: the essence of science consists not in the theories advanced at any one time but in the capacity to transform and replace those theories. Lévi-Strauss, of course, in seeing a connection between the way we view society and the way we view nature is not involved in crudities of this kind; he goes out of his way to insist that all our understanding of both nature and society is mediated by conceptual schemes, and that the conceptual schemes dominate our thinking, which in turn determines what we find meaningful and what we find problematic. Since the conceptual scheme is prior to our understanding of society, as well as to our understanding of nature, it cannot be a function of that understanding. Nevertheless the sophistication of Lévi-Strauss, as much as the crudity of Engels, entails a willingness to characterize as science an activity of theorizing which does not involve a continual attempt at the falsification of previously held theories.

As Mary Douglas has shown in her book *Purity and Danger*, primitive thought is characteristically reluctant to tolerate whatever is anomalous or exceptional to its own established classificatory schemes. Mrs. Douglas's investigation is aimed at explaining taboo rules and, more generally, rituals and rules pertaining to pollution and uncleanliness. Her thesis is that we misconstrue these rules if we look for underlying hygienic purposes or indeed if we interpret these rules as having any sort of utilitarian justification. When we do construe primitive rules in this way, we are projecting onto the primitive mind our awareness of pathogenic organisms, which is alien to it. The primitive's concept of dirt, of uncleanliness, is one of "matter out of place," of disorder. The unclean is that which violates his notion of order; his rites for dealing with pollution are techniques for preventing it from harming him; they enable him to recognize its existence and yet to resist revising or abandoning his beliefs and his conceptual schemes in the face of it. If we set Mrs. Douglas's analysis of the primitive mind beside Karl Popper's analysis of science, we immediately see that one view is the "photographic negative" of the other. Primitive man acknowledges the existence of the anomaly, of the exceptional, of that which constitutes a counterexample to his conceptual generalizations, only in order to outlaw that anomaly; and he thus avoids having to revise or reformulate his prevalent beliefs. The scientist, however, accepts anomalies and exceptions as a basis for either abandoning or revising the theories which he has hitherto accepted.

There is therefore a sharp line to be drawn between these two modes of thought, and I want to situate theism in relation to them. We can understand the logical structure of modern theism best if we see that in entering the modern world theism had to face two successive crises. These crises occurred for different social and cultural groups at different times, but the first crisis was most commonly experienced in the seventeenth or eighteenth century, the second in the nineteenth or twentieth. Moreover these crises, although they had an indirect impact upon the life of ordinary believers, were primarily crises for the theologically sophisticated. The first crisis had the following form. Theism was elaborated in the light of that prescientific culture where the anomalous and the exceptional are not permitted to falsify existing beliefs. Theism indeed marks a development of this mode of thought to a point at which irrefutability has been written into the content of the beliefs themselves, and is not just a characteristic of the manner in which they are professed and acted upon. The point is *not* that theistic beliefs are unfalsifiable in the sense in which some positivist philosophers have argued. Traditional theistic belief has factual content precisely because some episodes in the past (the history of Moses and Abraham, for example), some general features of the universe (the existence of life, for example), and some future states in an afterlife are held to be such that, had God not existed, things would not be or have been as they are. But all this is held together with the view that no set of phenomena could occur *now* (where *now* is whatever point in history we are at) of such a kind that their occurrence would show that God does not exist or that he lacks the fundamental attributes ascribed to him. While not therefore unfalsifiable in a positivist sense, theism is irrefutable in the Popperian sense, and the rise of science could not but create a crisis for it, the first of the two crises to which I have referred.

When the issue of refutability, the question of what

would falsify a given set of beliefs, is raised, the theist faces two alternatives. He may allow that his theism is "factual" in a perfectly ordinary sense, and he may exhibit the evidence which he thinks confirms his belief. In so doing, he assigns to his belief the status of a hypothesis: the belief acquires factual content at the cost of becoming vulnerable in just the way that any hypothesis is. If the belief is like the hypothesis of Newton's *Scholium*, for example—where God is required as the First Cause, which introduces motion into a system of material bodies every other aspect of which, including their relative motions, is explained in nontheological terms—then that belief is vulnerable to a Laplace, who has no need of it, or to a James Mill, who inquires why, if we require God as an external cause to account for the existence and character of the universe, we do not require a further cause to account for the existence and character of God. In other words, in a culture where refutability is admitted, theism can acclimatize itself by being reformulated as deism. Or it can refuse to acclimatize itself; and in so doing it must clearly segregate itself from the secular intellectual disciplines. Theology then becomes a realm apart, a discipline which legislates for itself and which disowns the current badges of intellectual legitimation; its links with general culture are necessarily weakened.

What I have called the first crisis in the modern history of theism amounted, then, to a debate over whether theism should adopt the strategy of converting itself into deism or that of separating itself from the secular culture. This crisis was not fully articulated by any one author; for the terms with which I have been able to characterize it are available to us now because we are spectators looking back after the event. But we find a partial consciousness of the dilemma in many writers, and what is most nearly a full consciousness of it is manifested in Pascal. Pascal resists the parceling out of God into separate functions the discharge of which is required for nature and society to be what they are. So he writes: "The God of Christians is not a God who is merely the author of mathematical truths and the order of the elements: that is the point of view of heathens and Epicureans" (*Pascal's Pensées*, tr. Martin Turnell [New York, Harper & Brothers, 1962], p. 115). And elsewhere in the same fragment (Lafuma fr. 17; Brunschvicg 556) he identifies this attitude explicitly with the deistic belief in a God who is an omnipotent cause. "They assume that [the Christian religion] consists simply in the worship of a God who is considered great and powerful and eternal; this properly speaking is deism, which is almost as far removed from the Christian religion as atheism, which is the exact opposite of it" (*Ibid.*, p. 114). It is precisely because he will not adhere to the deistic alternative that Pascal finds himself confronting the atheist in the name of a theism which is in no way refutable, and therefore in no way confirmable either.

Pascal, I suspect, treated atheism as a serious option for the first time in theistic history. Of course there had been atheistic precursors in the ancient world, but theism was left unscathed by them. The fool whom the Psalmist envisaged as saying "in his heart" that there is

no God was not when he spoke Hebrew denying that God existed but was supposing that God was temporarily absent. And St. Anselm's mistranslation of the impious Hebrew fool into an atheistic medieval Latin fool was still only speculative; atheism, for Anselm, was a logical possibility which theism had to consider, but not a live moral option which the theist had to fear as a serious rival. Pascal, however, in the dialogue of fragment 343 (Brunschvicg 233) of the *Pensées*, confronts an interlocutor who not only does not believe but is "so constituted that he cannot believe." Pascal, unlike Aquinas or John Locke, is able to find no arguments in the character of the universe to address to this man. All he can confront him with is a choice, the choice elaborated in his doctrine of the wager. Pascal's notion that theistic belief is something to be chosen is quite new in the history of theism. His innovation makes him the precursor of both Kierkegaard and Karl Barth; but he himself has no predecessors. Of course notions of choice are common enough in earlier theological writers, but there the choice is always between obedience—or allegiance—and disobedience to a given set of beliefs. What is new in Pascal is his exposition of the apparently paradoxical notion of "choosing to believe."

Thus, as a consequence of the first crisis theism was reformulated in alternative versions: one deistic; the other, to use an expression not available to its founding fathers, existentialist. The second crisis presupposed the first. What happened in the nineteenth century would be unintelligible if we did not know what happened in

the seventeenth. The second crisis occurred when theism in either of its new formulations was subjected to the critical standards of modern culture, which treats refutability as a necessary character of warrantable belief at every point in the study of history, in science, and in ordinary life. This has been the classic crisis of belief of the nineteenth and twentieth centuries. We may note three well-defined styles of response in that crisis. First, there was the response of those who rejected the deistic version of theism as James Mill rejected it. It was the reading of James Mill which discredited religious belief for the young Bertrand Russell, for example. In another case, it was recognizing the contingency of the world, its surdness—the inexplicability, in terms of any Leibnizian principle of sufficient reason, of why things as a whole should be as they are and not otherwise—that involved Sartre in atheism. Of such atheists we can ask, In which God is it that they disbelieve? In Russell's case it is the God of Newton's *Scholium*; in Sartre's case it is the God of Leibniz's *Theodicy*. The answers are characteristic: the God in whom the nineteenth and early twentieth centuries came to disbelieve had been invented only in the seventeenth century. But this type of atheist is quite different from the type with which we are more familiar today. The self-styled, free-thinking secularist societies of the nineteenth century—the backbone of those societies was often the self-educated working-class intellectual—used to lament that they recruited almost entirely from the ranks of the churches, and not at all from the masses of nonbelievers who surrounded them. The self-con-

scious ex-Christian atheist is thus to be distinguished from the secularized unbeliever, who sees no point in actually denying the existence of God because he never saw any point in affirming it in the first place. The first type of atheist continues to ask systematically the questions to which traditional theism gave answers. The second type no longer asks those questions; and to that extent his culture is impoverished. Individuals of the first type are sometimes the fathers of those of the second type. The children of active free-thinkers often lapse into a merely passive atheism—and this too was a continual complaint among the Victorian secularists. But the ranks of passive atheism are recruited over a much wider area, and to this point I shall revert later in the argument.

The second well-defined type of response to the deistic form of theism has been a total rejection of the attempt to adapt theism to the climate of secular thought, and an endeavor to preserve a theistic enclave in both thought and life. Rationally this response takes the form of insisting on the idiosyncrasy of religious concepts and beliefs. Culturally it sometimes takes the obvious form of emphasizing what theistic religions have in common rather than what divides them; this response is embodied not only in the Christian ecumenical movement but in the continual blurring of differences between Judaism and Christianity, and between both of these religions and other theisms, which is so characteristic of the contemporary churches. The concept of "the heathen" is something of an embarrassment to the modern theologian. In

the present day, even a Pope would be loath to inform
Hindus and Buddhists that they are in danger of going to
hell if they reject the gospel of Jesus Christ (although
this once was considered the most important message
that the Father of all Christians could deliver to non-
Christians). And yet, if orthodox Christianity is correct,
they are in that danger. Despite the utmost orthodox insistence on retaining the traditional creedal formulations, a process of "natural selection" seems to be occurring in which only some of the dogmas are really maintained with conviction while others, mere "vestiges," receive only the inconsequential deference of not being ex-
punged from the articles of faith.

The third form of response is to attempt to retain
Christian orthodoxy, to maintain a living relationship
between it and the culture of the world outside the
church, and yet to avoid the embarrassment of clashes
and conflicts between orthodox theism and contemporary secular culture. How can this be achieved? Precisely
by renouncing and denouncing contemporary secular
culture as a false culture. T. S. Eliot's social and political
writings are key texts here, although they are late addi-
tions to a tradition which derives from the Tractarians
and even has a source in Walter Scott. The popular response to Eliot ought to lead us to acknowledge that the
picture I have given of modern secular culture so far, inevitably brief and attenuated as it has been, suggests a
unity and a homogeneity which that culture does not in
fact possess. The self-conscious cultural atavism of Eliot
is not just a plea for a lost past; it is in part a plea for

those elements in the past still embodied in the present, for an identity that we can now neither fully recover nor yet quite disown.

If we look not at a largely church-going, albeit secularized, society, such as still exists in the United States, but at one where secularization has emptied the churches, as in England, we will be struck by the difference between the small proportion of the population who still profess orthodox Christian beliefs and practice their religion regularly and the much larger proportion who make use of the church only for the great occasions of the life-cycle: birth, marriage, death. This is one outstanding symptom that the secularization of the intellectual content of modern culture has not found anything like a total embodiment in moral and social behavior. Both the self-conscious intellectual atheists and the mass of passive nonbelievers, for example, believe that the death of a man's body is the end of that man. Yet this belief is not expressed in our way of reacting to death among our family or friends, except that we devise elaborate strategies, both in private and in public, to avoid acknowledging that a death has actually occurred. Either we are dumb or self-indulgent in our euphemisms, or we half pretend to be half-believers.

In the Victorian age, the debate about God lay at the focal point of both culture and morality. The epistemological standards and methods built up in both science and history confronted a theism which was still intimately connected with moral life. The question of whether theism was true could not be divorced from the question of what forms of morality were to be upheld. In asserting this fact, however, I am not accepting the contention of those Christian theologians who have argued that the abandonment of theistic belief inevitably leads to moral degeneration. That contention is just one possible answer to the question of what the relationship between theism and morality is, an answer which I shall examine in the next chapter. What I wish to stress here is that it was the very posing of the question about the relationship of Christianity to culture and to morals—rather than any particular answer given to the question —which marked the Victorian age. What is more, the question confronted the questioner with a problem which itself had some of the dimensions of a religious problem. In this respect the dispute about theism in the Victorian age was essentially similar to earlier episodes in the history of theism.

Paul Tillich maintained that secularization is not merely a process external to theism, with values opposed to those of theism, but that theism itself entails a drive toward secularization. For it is of the essence of theism to resist confusion between God and any feature of the world. Even Christ's human nature is to be sharply distinguished from his divine nature, according to Christian orthodoxy. The reverence accorded to Jesus the man (as distinguished from worship of him as God), so characteristic of modern Christianity, is heresy from that standpoint. Theism is not only to be distinguished from its post-Christian transformations; it is equally to be distinguished from all those pretheistic beliefs in which sacredness inheres in features of nature and society. The gods of the heathen are partially visible; the God of Abraham is wholly invisible. The consequent willingness of theists to recognize in increasing areas of human life the legitimate claims of secular standards is of some assistance in preventing conflict. Religion is able to withdraw from claims that it cannot uphold convincingly in the secular sphere. But now the point has been reached at which physics and politics—using both terms in their broadest sense—define a world in which theism has no place at all.

It may be objected that the schema which I have proposed for understanding the history of theism is one which totally fails to take account of the fact that theism encountered intellectual unbelief long before it encountered modern science and the modern study of history. To that objection I answer that the earlier unbelief which theism encountered, especially the unbelief of the ancient world, was something external to its own culture, and that insofar as it embodied an intellectual content—the content of ancient skepticism, for example—it used arguments to which there was a cogent form of reply. The tendency toward unbelief that posed a dilemma for men like Henry Sidgwick or Leslie Stephen, however, was part of the substance of his own culture, which he could not disown without disowning himself. The role of theism in Victorian life was conflict-creating; that role is lost now. One key reason why contemporary theism is not a live issue is that its apologetic efforts have been oversuccessful. The decrease in tension between Christianity and the secular disciplines is often greeted by theologians as a sign of a more favorable climate for Christianity. They perhaps ought to ask whether theism has lost a cultural role which lent it importance and relevance; whether theism, in participating in the disputes over biological evolution and the historical criticism of the New Testament, did not for the last time claim for itself the authority to sit in judgment upon secular culture. Can theism survive the renunciation of all such claims?

Durkheim's view that in worshiping its gods a society is worshiping itself in a disguised form has proved immensely fertile in the study of the religions of relatively primitive societies, but far less susceptible of easy application to the great theistic religions of relatively advanced societies. The reason for this, I believe, is that theism resists identification of the divine with forms of social life, as I have already mentioned. When theism rises and flourishes, it breaks the bonds which join the sacred and the secular; it cannot retain its own character and yet be wholly assimilated to the culture of a particular social group. If it is so assimilated, it ceases to be an external adversary and becomes instead merely an embodiment of the forms and values of whatever culture and society it happens to be situated in. In the past, of course, theism has often been partly assimilated. Only since the crisis of belief in the last century, however, has theism so emptied itself of any content that might affront us culturally that it has proved wholly assimilable. It has therefore reverted to the condition of those more primitive, pretheistic forms of religion to which Durkheim's thesis applies. This fact explains why secularization may follow either the Western European way of totally rejecting organized religion or the American way of not bothering to relinquish theism because to retain it involves so small a commitment. When religion is only thus able to retain its hold on society, religious belief tends to become not so much belief in God as belief in belief.

Belief in belief is sometimes thought in Europe to be a peculiarly American phenomenon, one articulated most strikingly in President Eisenhower's assertion that everybody should have a religious faith "and I don't care what it is." But I strongly suspect that in England—different as the religious situation appears there—among those who "believe," the same belief in belief flourishes. The difference is that the gap between what is said and what is meant is rather larger in England than it is in America. The English habit of oblique self-revelation is at once less apt than American forthrightness to produce damning evidence for quotation and more liable to invite the charge of hypocrisy. Belief in religious belief, as a substitute for belief in God, receives encouragement in both societies from a number of independent sources; one of which is psychoanalysis. Few psychoanalytic writers have gone as far as Jung in reinterpreting theism in this direction, but even Freudians have been found to participate in the enterprise. As Philip Rieff has pointed out, psychotherapy has too often come to substitute the question Will it be useful to believe this? for the question Is this belief true? (In so doing, of course, it betrays Freud in the most fundamental way.) Likewise, the political habit in Western nations of preserving religious formulas for use on public ceremonial occasions, by men of all beliefs or none, detaches the original meaning of these ceremonial formulas from the actual convictions of the men who utter them. Thus religious formulas tend increasingly to be used in modern society for purposes other than that of expressing the theological statements for which they were originally framed.

All these tendencies are evidence that contemporary theism, while retaining older forms, has very often changed the content which it invites us to believe or disbelieve. Moreover, contemporary theism has even altered the conception of what it is to believe or disbelieve. I can best exhibit this change by discussing two anomalous locutions I have had to use in characterizing recent theistic attitudes. I spoke earlier of Pascal, who urges upon us a "choice" between belief and unbelief; and I also spoke of the notion, in psychotherapy, of the "utility" of belief in certain things. Both of these locutions are anomalous with respect to the ordinary meaning of "believe" and its derivatives. Suppose that you ask me whether I believe it is going to rain tomorrow, and I reply that I do not know. Suppose that you then urge me to choose to believe it is going to rain tomorrow. I will be unable to do so, not because of any failure of effort but simply because anything that is summoned up by an act of will does not qualify as a belief—although it may qualify as a hope or a wish. This essential truth about the nature of "belief" is not really challenged by Pascal's advice that if only we will behave *as if* we believe, in time we shall come to believe. "Choosing to behave as if we believe" may be interpreted by some as "choosing to believe," but they are mistaken. Before I carry out the process of autosuggestion, I do not *choose* to believe, I simply *wish* that I did believe, and I therefore choose to do certain things; if the process of doing these things proves successful, I then believe. There is no moment of *choosing* to believe, despite what modern theologies influenced by existentialism might have us think. And there cannot be such a moment if what we are invited to believe in is what Pascal asks us to believe in, that is, the dogmas of Christian orthodoxy. For these dogmas are, or at least were, intended to be taken as factual truths in the same sense that it is a matter of fact whether or not tomorrow will bring rain. But if belief in truths of a factual kind cannot be chosen, then belief that can be chosen cannot have as its object truths of a factual kind. Therefore, if modern Christian theology treats Christian belief as belief that can be chosen, the truths of Christian orthodoxy must be regarded as something other than factual in kind.

Let us turn to the second anomalous locution I mentioned above, the "utility" of belief. What we recommend as useful cannot be thereby a proper object of belief. It may of course be very useful to believe that certain statements are true; but this utility can never be a reason for "believing" in them. I do not want to labor the logical point, however. Although philosophers who chide theologians—as I have just done—for logical or conceptual error in linking the notion of belief to notions of choice and utility are right on the conceptual point, they perhaps fail to diagnose properly what is being done by the theologians. For what is involved may be not so much an error about the traditional concept of belief as a correct insight into the transformation of that concept. If we do not note this possibility, we shall be less well able to understand how the debate between theism and atheism has become culturally marginal. For I am now in a position to answer, albeit only schematically, one of the questions which I posed at the outset of my argument: Is the cultural irrelevance, the marginal character, of the contemporary debate between atheism and theism merely due to the fact that the main advances of the secular disciplines no longer happen to be in areas in which a direct confrontation with theism occurs? My answer is that the lack of confrontation is due not only to the directions in which secular knowledge is advancing but to the directions in which theism is retreating. Theists are offering atheists less and less in which to disbelieve. Theism thereby deprives active atheism of much of its significance and power and encourages the more passive atheism of the indifferent. Thus the internal development of theism in response to the challenge of secular epistemological standards is an important factor in making the theism-versus-atheism dispute culturally marginal.

Yet the fact that the dispute between theists and atheists is now culturally marginal is itself significant for contemporary culture. With religious issues absent from the scene we are distanced not just from thinkers like Sidgwick and Leslie Stephen, but from George Eliot and Tolstoy too. Consequently, theologians as various as Dietrich Bonhoeffer, Rudolf Bultmann, and John Robinson in Europe; Paul Tillich, William Hamilton, and Paul Van Buren in America, have attempted to restate Christian theology so that it will be a vital issue. I view these attempts as a search for a new response to the second crisis of theism, a response which will neither reject the Christian religion nor retreat into a self-enclosed set of formulas (which we must totally accept or reject) nor attack contemporary secular culture in favor of self-conscious archaism. Neither Bertrand Russell nor Karl Barth nor T. S. Eliot, but . . . but what?

Common to the theologians I have mentioned is the project of distinguishing the kernel of Christian theism, which they believe can and must be detached from the outmoded husk. They may not agree among themselves as to the criteria for distinguishing the kernel from the husk, but they do agree ostensibly in accepting the substance of a modern secular standpoint in order to argue its compatibility with their faith. For Van Buren perhaps the key element in that standpoint is modern linguistic philosophy; for Hamilton it is (as it was earlier for Bonhoeffer) scientific and technical achievement, which has eroded the former sense of creaturely dependence; for others, other elements of secular culture are important.

But each of these theologians requires that his own restatement of Christian theism shall both distinguish the theistic kernel from the theistic husk and be intelligible to contemporary educated, secular-minded men. I maintain, however, that these aims are essentially incompatible with each other; that any presentation of theism which is able to secure a hearing from a secular audience has undergone a transformation that has evacuated it entirely of its theistic content. Conversely, any presentation which retains such theistic content will be unable to secure the place in contemporary culture which those theologians desire for it. I am thus advancing not merely the weaker contention that all their attempts so far have failed but the stronger contention that any attempt of this kind must inevitably fail.

Consider a number of examples of different kinds: Bultmann's revision of the Christian doctrine of salvation consists of identifying the Christian choice between redemption and damnation with the Heideggerian choice between authentic and inauthentic existence. Kamlah, Bultmann's student, has in turn argued that, if Bultmann's identification is correct, then Jesus Christ is important only because he happened to anticipate Heidegger in uttering a true doctrine, the truth of which, and our ground for believing in the truth of which, is quite independent of the truth of Christian orthodoxy. But if this is so, then the historical Jesus must lack the kind of importance which orthodox Christianity has ascribed to him. I shall waive the question of whether Heideggerian interpretations of Christianity are likely to be any more intelligible to us than traditional ones, and shall simply say that Kamlah is so clearly right on this key point that he raises for us in the most insistent way the question of why Bultmann is able to think of himself as a Christian at all. The answer may be that Bultmann tacks onto his doctrine an entirely traditional belief in the existence and nature of God; the link between the modernized formulations embodied in his demythologizing of the New Testament and this traditional theism is unstated, and indeed must remain so. The content of Bultmann's theology, then, falls into two categories: that which is made credible ceases to be theistic, and that which remains theistic is not made credible in any way.

In the theology of Tillich we find perhaps not so much a simple dichotomy, like Bultmann's, as an oscillation. Tillich uses traditional theistic language—the characterization of God as "the ground of being," for example—and an existentialist metaphysics to provide a framework for this vocabulary. But when he explains his concept of God to the lay mind; he identifies God with man's ultimate concern. His freedom to pass from the metaphysical concept to the psychological (and transitions between the metaphysical and the psychological are at the very core of Tillich's thought) is at least partly secured by the fact that he characterizes the metaphysical entity in almost purely negative terms. This reduces the positive characterization of God to human psychological terms: "God" is a name given to human concern. But this psychological reduction is exactly what was called atheism in the nineteenth century by Feuerbach, who held the view that theistic language is not without a real referent, albeit a purely human one. For Feuerbach this position entailed the apparently obvious conclusion that theistic language is systematically inappropriate for atheism; that to decipher its true meaning prompts abandoning its use. However, Tillich, whose decipherment was reasonably similar to Feuerbach's, saw no reason for reaching Feuerbach's conclusions. Why this change? Precisely, I believe, because of the whole change in the cultural climate, in the character of theism, and in the relation between the two, which I described earlier. The theism in which Feuerbach disbelieved underwent a sea change into the theism in which Tillich believed. Not only are Tillich and Bultmann to be understood in terms of this historical change, but their writing in turn provides evidence about the character of that change.

To turn to a quite different part of the theological spectrum, consider Van Buren's doctrine. Van Buren represents the extreme point in the sacrifice of theistic content. He wishes to preserve Christian language and practice, but without commitment to anything traditionally recognized as belief in the existence of God. Prayer—although it uses expressions which would naturally be construed as addressed to an external deity, to whom praise, petition, and thanksgiving might be appropriate—becomes a technique for orienting and transforming the self. But what Van Buren fails to recognize is that prayer must then be judged as such a technique, competing with other like techniques, notably psychoanalysis. And we have little reason to believe that it would compete successfully. Or rather, in order that it might so compete, its practitioners would have to learn from the experience of the analytic therapies. Prayer would then be transformed into a therapy, and the gap between the theistic formula recited and its nontheistic application would become at best a gross embarrassment. That is, prayer would be absorbed totally into the family of secular analytic therapies. (One might say that in Jungian theory and practice, something rather like this has already happened.) Thus the abandonment of theistic content in favor of secular intelligibility leads away from even the remnants of theistic practice.

The new theologies, then, turn out to be symptoms of the very disease for which they profess to be the cure. But why does this concern those of us who are not theists? In part because of a feature of the Victorian debate about God which I have so far taken into little account. Nineteenth-century theists as different as Gladstone and Dostoyevsky were haunted by the fear that the loss of theistic belief would result in moral collapse. Our contemporary theologians, with their quite new style, still wish to preserve that part of the kernel of Christian belief which is concerned with morality. Presumably they fear, as their predecessors did, that an entirely secularized world may lose the distinctive moral contribution of Christian theism. But are their fears justified? To this topic, which clearly requires a more extended treatment, I shall turn in the following chapter.

Atheism and Morals

ALMOST ALL
the great skeptics and atheists of the modern Western
world have been morally conservative, often intensely so,
in their lives as well as in their teachings. To Freud and
Marx, for example, who took many of the traditional virtues for granted, the unorthodox moral behavior and attitudes of many Marxists and Freudians would have
been highly distasteful. On the other hand, many Christian theists have played their part in the great crimes of
the age: devout Catholics were among the guards of the
Nazi concentration camps; and believing Protestants
participated in the bombings of Hiroshima and Dresden.
In view of these facts, the Dostoyevskian contention
that if God does not exist everything is permitted must
necessarily appear difficult to maintain.

But, my opponents may retort, the Dostoyevskian
contention applies only in the long run. Their argument
might go as follows: Lacking a belief in God, men lack
an essential justification for morality, a justification
which is necessary, although not alone sufficient, to en-
sure moral behavior. This necessity is not evident in the

first or second generation of atheists, still in close contact with the traditions of theism (Freud's father brought him up on the Bible, Marx was the grandson of a rabbi, and James Mill began his career as a minister of the Church of Scotland). But their children's children (the number of generations need not be specified) will inevitably exhibit a decline in moral standards and behavior. As one influential image has it, the "moral capital" built up through centuries of theistic belief and practice will be gradually dissipated as secular life develops.

I believe that this image is inappropriate and I question whether belief in God furnishes an essential justification for morality. I do not intend here to discuss whether the promise of rewards or the threat of punishments in a future life does in fact furnish an effective motive for moral behavior. What I am principally concerned with here are the logical connections between belief in God and morality; my contention is that theism itself requires and presupposes both a moral vocabulary which can be understood independently of theistic beliefs and moral practices which can be justified independently of theistic beliefs.

I take it to be characteristic of theism—as contrasted with pretheistic religions—that God is no longer thought to have an exclusively local habitation. Particular loci on the earth—whether the tangible elements used in the sacraments, or the Holy of Holies in the temple—may in some special sense be considered dwelling places of the divine, but God is regarded as the God of all the earth. As such, he wills a way of life distinguishable from that embodied in the social system of any particular community. That is, theism must deal with the question of the right rules for all men to live by and the true goods for all men to pursue. For this question theism must rely on the critical use of an evaluative vocabulary—the more particularly since the divine will must be both appealed to in the criticism of humanity and commended to humanity as well. The evaluative vocabulary must be used in the formulation of central theological statements, when goodness is ascribed to God and obedience to him declared to be a virtue. But if these statements are to have any substantial content, then expressions such as "good," "virtue," and the like must be defined in terms the use of which does not presuppose theistic beliefs. To put it very crudely, we ought to do what God commands, if we are theists, because it is right in some independent sense of "right," rather than hold that what God commands is right just because God commands it, a view which depends upon "right" being defined as "being in accordance with what God commands." To this it may be retorted that I am arguing that the former of these two views is logically required by the character of theism and the latter view excluded, but that this cannot be so, just because many theists in fact think otherwise. For there is a well-known theological view according to which the use of evaluative terms within theism *must* be idiosyncratic and the meaning of these terms must involve a reference to the will of God. When we call God good, we cannot on this view mean what we mean when we call men good; the standards embodied in the vocabulary of our ordinary human evaluative discourse are the standards of a fallen, sinful race. This is the explicit or implicit position of many Protestants; both Luther and Kierkegaard seem committed to it in at least *some* of their writings. And it has its roots in the theological ethics of medieval nominalism. What I wish to show is that this view is internally incoherent, and the most vivid way in which I can begin to show this is by pointing out that it is difficult, if this view is correct, for theists to distinguish between God and the devil in the way that they must. For if "God is good" and "We ought to do whatever God commands" are transformed into tautologies by means of redefinitions of "good" and "right," it follows that we can have no moral reasons for obedience to divine commandments. All apparently reason-backed injunctions of the form "Do this because God commands it and what God commands is right and obedience to his commands produces certain goods" collapse into injunctions in which "Do this because God commands it" is merely being reiterated in certain disguised and misleading ways. But if we cannot have this kind of reason for obedience to divine commandments, what other type of reason can there be for such obedience but the appeal to divine power and to the consequences of flouting it? It is at this point that the differences between God and the devil are blurred. For God has been transformed by the proponents of this view into a Hobbesian sovereign whose title to legitimate authority rests not on his absolute paternal care, his goodness as a father, but solely on his power, and the devil's lack of such a title rests solely on his inferiority in respect of power. Satan becomes a Hobbesian rebel who fails to be a Hobbesian sovereign only because he is unsuccessful. Christian theism in particular can scarcely tolerate this: to cite only one example, the story of the temptation of Jesus by Satan with the offer of all the kingdoms of the world loses its point even as a parable unless God and Satan stand in a different moral relationship to power, in a sense of "moral" which is our ordinary familiar sense.

It follows from this that theism, if it is to be coherent, must rely for its statement upon an independently understood moral vocabulary. To this conclusion, I now wish to add another and stronger thesis; namely, that theistic practice depends upon the existence of independent moral practices. I can bring out what I mean by drawing an analogy with the status of a legal code. One may have two quite different types of reason for obeying a given law; for example, a law that prohibits theft. One type of reason is that which appeals to the point or purpose of the prohibition, in this case to the advantages to be gained by each and all from the institution of stable property. The other type of reason is that which appeals to the penalties prescribed for disobedience to the law. A legal code which arbitrarily ordains and prohibits actions that are without reasonable point or purpose commands our allegiance only insofar as it is able to deploy power to enforce its sanctions. As with legal codes in general, so also with divine law. If God's commands are not to be mere fiats backed by arbitrary power then they must command actions which can be seen to have point and purpose independent of, and antecedent to, the divine utterance of divine law. The practice of making evaluative, and indeed moral, judgments of actions must be such that it can have been preexistent to theistic moral injunctions. These conceptual points were clearly well understood in a great deal of medieval theology and especially in the thought of Aquinas, but they can be divorced from any specific commitment to Aristotelianism. They cannot be divorced, however, from the requirement that morality be understood in a particular way, be seen in a particular light. Not only does theism require an independently conceived moral vocabulary and preexistent moral practices, but these must be of a certain kind. This requirement may have gone unnoticed in the past because what theism requires morality to be is in fact what morality has been traditionally taken for. A key contention of my argument, however, is that morality is of this kind no longer.

What morality is required to be by theism and what it usually has been considered to be is a set of rules which are taken as given and are seen as having validity and authority independent of any external values or judgments. It is essential to morality so conceived that we accept the rules wholly and without question. We must not seek rational grounds for accepting them, nor can we decide, on rational grounds, to revise them—although we may discover by chance that we were mistaken in what we thought the content of the rules to be. When morality is considered in this light, theories about morality are accounts of why the code of moral rules includes the items that it does and no others. Platonic and Aristotelian morality both offer theories of this kind. Aristotelianism grounds its explanation in the view that human nature has certain inherent goals, needs, and wants. The cogency of this theoretical explanation depends on the fact that the society which upholds the given moral rules agrees upon a way of life defined in terms of just those goals, wants, and needs. When I speak of a morality in which moral rules are taken as given I do not mean to imply that this morality may not coexist with certain justifying and explanatory theories. I do not even mean to imply that those who live by such a morality are necessarily unaware that alternative moral codes and practices may exist. But I do hold that morality of this kind is such that these convictions underpin it: first, that the content of the morality is at least as well justified as, and probably better justified than, any particular theory about morality; second, that although the morality actually adhered to at any time may be discrepant from the one true morality, the discrepancy is only marginal; and, therefore, that any theory of morality which suggests the currrent moral beliefs are fundamentally mistaken is automatically discredited. This attitude toward morality is compatible with a variety of moral beliefs and has prevailed in a variety of social contexts; of itself it entails no particular content for morality, only a particular kind of allegiance to the current morality, whatever it is. In fact, since the medieval period, this attitude has outlived in the Western world a number of different contents for morality. This becomes particularly evident in the closing phases of its history—which are still with us, but which began much earlier. Thinkers as radical as Hume and John Stuart Mill are noteworthy for their insistence —except for a few particular moral questions (Hume on suicide, for example, and Mill on birth control)—that their utilitarianism, far from being at odds with current moral beliefs, provides both an explanation and an endorsement of them. The contrast between Bentham and Mill is instructive here. Bentham's whole emphasis in discussing the criterion of utility is upon the clash with established opinion. Mill, however, insists that, the criterion of utility, rightly understood, is consistent with the largest part of what we have always believed.

The relation of theism to morality of this kind is uncomplicated. Theism furnishes an explanation for the authority and the fixed character of the rules, both by according them divine status and by providing grounds for the underlying belief in a single determinate human nature. God created men with just those goals, wants, and needs which a way of life embodying the given rules will enable them to achieve. To the natural morality of men theism adds rules concerned with man's supernatural end, and a set of beliefs and practices concerning guilt, repentance, and forgiveness to provide for moral, as well as religious, failure. Theism and morality of this kind naturally and easily reinforce one another. I think, moreover, that theologians have this kind of morality in mind when they assert that the loss of theistic belief will bring about, or has brought about, a loss of m... ...ty. My central thesis is the direct opposite of their view: I hold not that a loss of theistic belief produces a loss of moral belief and a change of practice but rather that a change in the character of morality is at least partly responsible for the modern inability to accept theistic belief. That is, I wish to invert the Dostoyevskian contention about the relation between theism and morals.

So far I have argued that theism presupposed and needed for its own statement and practice one particular type of attitude to morality. In support of my main thesis, I now add that this traditional attitude to moral rules, which theism presupposed and required, has decayed for a number of reasons which are independent of, and largely prior to, our loss of theistic belief. These reasons can be set out in only roughly chronological order because their historical interrelationship has yet to be adequately chronicled.

The first of these causes was the impact of those versions of Christianity—mainly Protestant, but in some cases Catholic—according to which human nature is seen as so corrupt that human morality must be considered of no account. The consequence of this view is that from any human standpoint the divine commandments do become arbitrary fiats imposed on us externally; our nature does not summon us to obey them, because we cannot recognize them as being for our good. The motives of hope of eternal reward and fear of eternal punishment then must completely replace temporal motives for morality. There are two versions of this Protestant ethic. The first is the one with which Weber familiarized

us, according to which it is true at one and the same
time that the realm of secular economic life is allowed to
become autonomous in its norms precisely because it is
not the realm of salvation and damnation and yet that
success in that realm is taken to be an outward sign of
inward redemption. We are almost overfamiliar with the
process of secularization that ensued; but insufficiently
familiar with the fact that as many texts from Luther
could be cited in an account of the origins of an ethic of
divine arbitrariness which coexisted with the first.
Where Franklin's *Autobiography* is a classic text for the
study of the development of the ethic of work, James
Hogg's novel *The Memoirs of a Justified Sinner* is the
classic text for this kind of antinomianism. The hero—or
rather the protagonist—of Hogg's novel has been taught
to believe that the blood of Christ covers all his sins, because he is of the elect; he concludes that he may therefore sin without limit. He can envisage no possible reason for restraint upon his actions other than that which
would derive from the fear of retribution. His theism has
left him moralityless. Clearly Hogg portrays a character
in whom a tendency present in real life has been carried
to an extreme to which it is never or rarely carried in that
life—just as Dostoyevsky does with Raskolnikov. But the
very tendency is equally plainly one that undermines
morality as hitherto understood.

A second tendency also inimical to that morality was
that embodied in the liberal principle that the individual
is sovereign within the sphere of morality. In classical
liberalism this principle is often and significantly ex-

pressed in an incoherent form. For it is first of all presented as itself an objective truth whose moral validity
and authority in no way depend upon individual moral
agents' assenting to it or deciding to make it their own;
and yet since the right that it ostensibly confers upon the
individual is an unrestricted right to make his own decisions as to what principles shall be binding upon him, it
is a self-destructive principle. Certainly the picture derived from it of each individual as uttering moral injunctions to himself which gain their authority from no
source other than his own will and choice is inconsistent
with the morality that theism requires. Kant's moral philosophy will provide us with illumination at this point,
for Kant wrote at a key period for the history of the relations between theism and morality, when the rift between them had become clearly apparent, and morality
had half, but only half, changed its character. It is an
undergraduate-essay commonplace that Kantian ethics is
riddled with incoherences. The possibility that is treated
with inadequate seriousness is that Kant was not in fact
for the most part the incoherent and inconsistent analyst
of a set of coherent and consistent moral concepts, implied in the practice and utterance of ordinary moral
agents, but rather that Kant was the coherent and consistent recorder and analyst of an incoherent and inconsistent set of moral concepts which were embodied in an
incoherent and inconsistent moral practice, and one that
had become so as a consequence of the very tendencies
which I have been noting. Kant, if we read him thus,
provides us with confirmatory evidence on a number of

matters. The autonomy of morality he recognizes when he asserts that men cannot derive it from theism if they are to call God or "the Holy One of Israel" good in any significant sense; yet he still invokes a theistic explanation to give morality point. He must do so, since for Kant the heterogeneity, the variety, the incompatibility, which mark man's natural goals, needs, and wants entail that these can provide us with no stable criteria. He cannot find, as the medieval Aristotelian would, any point or proof for morality in terms of the satisfaction of the needs and wants of a human nature created by God to be of a certain determinate kind; and he invokes theism only as an assurance that goodness will be rewarded in another life. While theism is assigned this attenuated role, the autonomous moral agent is presented as one whose moral prescriptions have no authority other than that derived from himself as a rational agent and yet have the character of a law.

But what authority can a law have which I utter to myself? And what sanction can a law have of which I am expressly told that there are no earthly sanctions to back it and when the theistic sanction is invoked to make morality theoretically intelligible rather than to provide one with a motive? In other words, in Kant's writings the notion of morality as a law, and with it the traditional notion of one true morality, is combined with a liberal individualist recognition of the individual's sovereignty, and so is considered as a law only in some rather curious sense at best; and this unstable combination was indeed bound to lead to a victory for the liberal indivi ualist elements of the conceptual scheme and a defeat for those elements derived from the traditional ways of regarding morality. And this is because these matters were not merely episodes in the intellectual history of theology and philosophy, but stood in intimate relationship to what was happening in society at large. For the morality that had become so irrelevant in theory was having its roots in social practice destroyed by a rate and type of social change which made ordinary men far more conscious of the actual and potential variety of competing and conflicting moralities and ways of life and the need to choose between them, and thus it was undermining the notion of one true morality.

It is a common observation of social history that the industrial working class in Western Europe did not leave the churches at any point, because it had never entered them. The industrial working class was formed in a new environment, outside the type of community in which the traditional view of morality was upheld and theism still made sense. Urbanization and industrialization produced a new form of social life, in which religious utterance and activity were necessarily contextless gestures. Other reasons may be offered to explain why the moral education of those who developed in such an environment was never theistic; for example, in many industrial communities there were neither churches nor pastors. But I argue that even where the church was present the moral beliefs necessary to theism were lacking, as much among nonintellectuals as among intellectuals.

As a result of the tendencies I have described, two beliefs have come to be the unexpressed assumptions of much moral debate. The first of these beliefs is that disagreements between rival moral views are essentially irreconcilable, that there are no shared criteria to which men may appeal in order to settle fundamental disputes. In the twentieth century this belief has been articulated in philosophical theories as different as the emotivism of C. L. Stevenson and the existentialism of Sartre. The moral practice and utterance which Stevenson and Sartre analyze, however, is not traditional moral practice and utterance but the moral practice and utterance of a culture which came into existence only with the death of belief in a single determinate human nature, belief to which a single moral code was appropriate. The obvious counterpart to the idea that fundamental moral disputes are in principle irreconcilable is the belief that there is not just a single determinate human nature; that human nature is immensely malleable; and that around the relatively unchanging biological core society and culture may weave very different patterns, resulting in widely varying wants, needs, and goals. It is just because this belief is dominant now that no ultimate shared criteria can be invoked by which moral disputes may be resolved.

Theism has lost the morality which it logically presupposed; and the lack of social contact between theism and contemporary morality is at least partly to be explained by the lack of logical connection between theistic beliefs and modern moral beliefs. The response to this situation of course produces those tendencies which I remarked in the first chapter—tendencies to retreat into a closed or-

thodoxy or a doctrine of arbitrary choice or cultural atavism. It is thus not only the intellectual but also the
moral climate created by science and technology that has
transformed theism into an alien cult. The modern
moral climate confronts theism with dilemmas parallel
to those produced by the intellectual climate. It is perhaps not uncharacteristic of the United States and Great
Britain that American versions of the new theology
have been dominantly concerned with intellectual issues,
and British versions rather more concerned with moral
issues. The new morality is not just a concomitant, but
a very substantial part, of the new theology; in fact,
when more traditional versions of theism are demytholo-
gized, morality is sometimes alleged to represent the
heart of religion. The new theistic morality is usually
concerned with personal problems, such as sexual relationships, rather than with political problems like war.
That theistic morality should be least at home with
moral problems embedded in the very structure of our
communal lives is itself damaging; but even more damaging is the content of the answers which the new theistic morality does try to provide.

Consider the two poles of the new sexual morality represented by the views of John Robinson, the bishop of
Woolwich; and the Commission of the British Council
of Churches. Robinson abandons the traditional forms
of justifying Christian attitudes to sexuality; nonetheless,
he wishes in effect to preserve the traditional rules. The
Commission of the British Council of Churches, in its
report on sexual morality, abandons both the traditional

attitudes and the traditional justifications. Robinson officially abjures the legalistic form of morality (the traditional concept of moral law) and declares his allegiance to a morality guided by the motive of love; but he further maintains that a man who acts from this motive will necessarily abstain from sexual relations outside marriage. His conclusion can be correct only if the traditional rules are covertly reintroduced into his definition of the word "love." Since Robinson has rejected all traditional forms of justification for the traditional rules, however, his adhesion to the rules consequently appears arbitrary and irrational. Of the Commission's position on sexual morality, one might say that it is either untrue or impertinent. The contention that sexual relationships outside marriage are permissible in exceptional cases cannot be true unless traditional Christianity is false; but if traditional Christianity is false, then the Commission ought to admit that it is now announcing to the secular world, as though by way of a discovery, what the secular world has been announcing to it for a rather long time.

The inconsistencies of modern theistic morality might be presented as adding weight to an argument against theism from a secular, atheistic standpoint. To do so would be misguided, however, as we see if we turn our consideration from the gap between theism and the contemporary theistic morality to the gap between the prophecies of the great eighteenth- and nineteenth-century secularists and the present-day secular morality. The refutation of theistic belief was presented by those thinkers as a form of liberation for the human spirit. An irrational, superstitious world view was to be replaced by a rational, progressive one. The strangling of the last king with the entrails of the last priest was to celebrate a marriage between new social forms, in which men would determine their own destiny and beliefs, beliefs by means of which they would understand their true place in the world. If the moral rhetoric of theism has become disembodied, the moral rhetoric of this kind of secularism has scarcely achieved incarnation at all—for not dissimilar reasons.

The majority of secular moralities are versions of utilitarianism; and all versions of utilitarianism suffer from their distortion of the key term, "utility," and of those terms, such as "happiness" and "pleasure," which have been employed as substitutes for it. The word "utility" was originally used with a narrower meaning and in a narrower set of contexts than now associated with it by utilitarians. Their use of the word to mean a general criterion by which rival claims upon an individual may be weighed against one another presupposes the prior identification of a homogeneous set of goals, needs, and wants among all men. As I have already pointed out, however, in modern life such an identification can take place only within very limited areas. Our range of disagreement over what principles to profess and what actions to perform is symptomatic of the wide diversity of goals, wants, and needs which marks contemporary human nature. The good for man cannot be defined in terms of agreement in wants, even in long-term wants, because our wants are various and mutable.

This inability to frame general moral notions and general moral criteria has all the graver consequences because it occurs in an age when moral particularity has been left behind. Indeed the need for general notions and criteria springs from that fact. In referring to a loss of "moral particularity," I mean that those concepts of virtue which were tied to particular occupations and statuses have been submerged. Concepts such as "duty" and "obligation" will illustrate the point. These notions originally had a highly specific force: "duties" belonged to a particular office or status; "obligations" arose out of either status or contractual relationships. What duties a man had was a question of fact, directly and clearly determined by the offices he held and his position in society. What obligations a man was under was equally a question of fact, the consequence of his social status and the contracts which he had entered into. Gradually these pluralistic concepts of "duties" and "obligations" have been superceded by notions of "Duty" and "Obligation." The concepts have been evacuated of particular references to the facts of social life and have been generalized into near synonyms for what a man ought to do not as a holder of this or that particular office or status but as a man.

This generalization of the moral vocabulary is of course connected with the rise of individualism, which attempts to separate what a man is in essence from what appear to be mere contingencies of kinship, status, and occupation. It is thus a process dependent on some of the other elements which I have noted as agents in the corrosion of traditional morality. Entailed in the process of generalization, we should recognize, is the impoverishment of the moral vocabulary. "Pleasure," "utility," and "happiness" are concepts which once could be plainly distinguished; within a secular utilitarian framework their differences become blurred. "Duty" and "obligation" suffer similarly. The criteria for discriminating between virtues and vices become unclear. I suggest that this process of moral generalization is disconcerting, not only to theists but also to any would-be successor to the prophets of atheism and secularism—from the French *philosophes*, through Marx, to Freud. The factors contributing to this process I have of necessity listed in an unsystematic way. Systematization would have involved a sociological theory of culture and of religion's place in it which we are only beginning to formulate, as well as a historical narrative which has yet to be written.

I have been working hitherto in an uncritical way with the category of morality, as though it were absolutely defined and always distinguishable from other categories, such as aesthetics, politics, and religion. Such a categorization is implicit in my discussion of the relations between theism and morality. But there have of course been societies in the past to which this particular range of categories cannot be accurately applied. In the Icelandic society portrayed in the sagas, for example, the moral structure and the social structure are one and the same thing—a fact vividly exemplified by the word *skyldr* (the source of our "should"), which is used to express both a state of kinship and a state of obligation.

The two ideas are fused into one within the Icelandic conceptual scheme. So complete is the identification of morality with the social structure that morality provides no means of criticizing that social structure. Can we then rightly go on talking of it as "morality"? Only if we are careful not to imply that morality is an autonomous category there as it is in some other societies. The societies to which this kind of categorization may be applied are those where morality is an autonomous or semi-autonomous realm. If my earlier argument is correct, they are those societies where theism flourishes or which still live in the shadow of theism. But if the later part of my argument is correct, morality in our own posttheistic society has collapsed into its neighbors—to use Hegel's vivid metaphor of the ballet of the categories (the dance is, as Hegel pointed out, a drunken one). What is the nature of this collapse and what has taken morality's place? Perhaps it does not matter much at this point whether we speak of morality as changing its character or as being replaced. The latter formulation, however, may invite us to ignore the extent to which the categories that have assimilated morality are themselves transformed by the assimilation. At least two of these categories are important.

The first of these is the organizational category. When histories of morality are written, they do not usually refer to the topics included by sociologists in works about organization theory; equally organization theorists do not usually refer us back to the history of morals. But as more and more of life is bureaucratized and as informal

organizations, and informal procedures within formal organizations, are affected by their bureaucratic context,
more and more of the decisions which once belonged to
areas of social life outside the sphere of organization
come within it. Seymour Martin Lipset has remarked in
relation to politics that bureaucratization more and more
removes decisions from the realm of ends to that of
means, converts areas of moral disagreement into areas
of technical disagreement. But what Lipset does not re-
mark is that the area of technical disagreement may be
changed in the process. For men now seem to identify
themselves with issues of procedure or technique more
than they once did. If this is so, commitment acquires a
quite new style, and the organizational milieu a different
type of moral importance. I am not here accepting the
banal thesis of White's *The Organization Man;* indeed I am suggesting almost the opposite. The work of
Christopher Argyris, for example, shows that a tension
exists between the suppression of personal emotions,
which the rational decision-making procedure of an organization generally requires, and the development of
personal sensitivity and sensibility, which effective par-
ticipation in the organization demands. As Argyris demonstrates, effective organizations are forced to breed virtues they cannot entirely accommodate and which provide their members with a moral standing-ground that is
to some degree independent of the organization's imme-
diate needs—as seen by those in control—although it is
inseparable from the organizational milieu. That is, we
have here neither the complete identification of moral

and social structure which is found in some relatively simple societies nor that categorical distinctiveness so characteristic of an earlier phase of our own culture but a more complex interrelationship. It is not surprising that the morality of organizations has been misperceived, from an older moral standpoint, as a mere mass conformism, for here we have not only a new content but a new style.

The word "style" significantly brings us to a second category with which morality has blended, that of the aesthetic. Not what you say but how you say it; how you look as you say it, or what type face you publish it in; what badges you exhibit for recognition by others; the purity or impurity of response to these badges: all these values infect the substance of contemporary urbanized relationships. Much is at stake for the individual in the matter of style; failure or success in it may cost him a great deal. Aesthetics has acquired a new moral dimension, morality has been aestheticized.

All of this creates a climate in which it is difficult to raise the questions theism traditionally answered. The morality which both the questions and the answers presupposed is lacking to a great degree; and to that degree the questions and the answers have become unintelligible. For those whose lives embody the new moral forms, furthermore, the forms are not apt to raise general questions about the nature of man and morality. The morality of style is perhaps most obviously untheoretical; to ask theoretical questions about ultimate justifications is to move away from aesthetic values and would seem, to those who live by such values, an attempt to break a butterfly upon a wheel. For the individual agent, however, the morality of organizational procedures is always bounded by the horizons of the organizations to which he belongs. The scope of traditional religion and morality is lacking. What does this entail for the new theologians and for the atheist?

In my opinion, the new theologian is faced—as I argued in the first chapter—with this disconcerting fact: the demythologizing of the Gospel and the proclamation that God (or at least the idea of God) is absent or dead leave him unable to claim that his faith is either intellectually or morally distinctive. Just as Bultmann has been shown by Kamlah to be nothing but a Heideggerian except for his vocabulary; just as Tillich's definition of God in terms of ultimate human concern in effect makes of God no more than an interest of human nature, so the new morality is seen to consist in reality either of arbitrary, unintelligible dogma or of familiar secular practice. The new theism turns out to be in morals as in theology the project of retaining a religious vocabulary emptied of belief-content. But before the atheist scorns this overmuch, he ought to ask what light the situation throws on his own predicament. The inclination of the new theology to retain the traditional religious vocabulary must be due partly to the failure of atheists to provide a vocabulary for the traditional religious and moral questions. Indeed, as other writers have observed, even the ideologies that have provided a limited contemporary secular vocabulary for such questions tend to relapse into religious forms—I refer to psychoanalysis in particular, but also to Marxism. The key developments I have tried to identify in our culture have placed not only theism but also its atheistic critics in a position where their debates cannot supply contemporary cultural needs. We must recognize the centrality of this fact in our cultural analysis.

My total argument has drawn support from academic disciplines as various as philosophy, history, literature, and the sociological theory of organization. (This in itself is a reflection of the cultural situation which I have been examining.) I have tried to outline a method of inquiry; my assertions have been framed primarily with an eye to suggesting questions, rather than to giving answers. Since the points which I have adduced from such a broad area of human knowledge all deserve closer scrutiny, I cannot but regard my argument and conclusions as largely provisional. This brief inquiry, then, is the beginning of an investigation, rather than the end.

On at least one point, however, I hope that my conclusion is clearly seen to be more than provisional. Both the atheist and the theist are trying to answer the same question. However much they may dispute about the answers, they agree about the importance of the question. Both, moreover, are trying to function in a culture and society inimical to them and uninterested in their debate. And, as I have suggested before, an understanding of the marginal position of their debate in our culture is a key to our understanding of both that culture and ourselves.

In the nineteenth century Robertson Smith was accused of heresy by his Scottish Presbyterian ministerial peers because he insisted on investigating the Old Testament from an anthropological standpoint. What worried his colleagues was something that they themselves did not, and perhaps could not, make wholly explicit; that is, Smith's tendency to see beliefs in a social context and to ask not Are they true? but Why should men in that sort of society hold that sort of belief? We experience little discomfort when we view the beliefs of the Nuer or the Azande peoples in this way, since nothing is at stake for us in the truth or error of their beliefs. But when we focus on our own beliefs we find it difficult to go on asking both questions simultaneously. I have tried to view the debate between atheists and theists as if I were an anthropologist from another culture. Would indeed that we were able wholly to adopt such a standpoint; then we might acquire the kind of objectivity that would enable us to distinguish between temporary cultural fashion and long-term cultural trends. Anyone who considers this debate must always fear that he has not taken sufficient account of that important distinction.

Religion, Atheism,
and Faith

PAUL RICŒUR

Religion, Atheism,
and Faith

THE TOPIC "THE
Religious Significance of Atheism" presents me with a
fundamental challenge. I must say how far I am able to
recognize and to adopt for my own thinking the critique
of religion generated by such atheists as Nietzsche and
Freud, and to what extent I consider that I, as a Christian, am beyond the ordeal of religious doubt. As I see it,
the phrase "the religious significance of atheism" suggests that atheism does not exhaust itself in the negation
and destruction of religion; rather, that atheism clears
the ground for a new faith, a faith for a postreligious age.
Such is the working hypothesis which I hope to vindicate
in this brief inquiry. The subtitle I have chosen—"Religion, Atheism, and Faith"—expresses my intention fairly
well. I have placed "atheism" in an intermediary position; for I wish to consider it as both a break and a link
between religion and faith. I am aware of the difficulties
of this viewpoint. We must not take the distinction between religion and faith for granted. Nor should we use
atheism as an indiscreet form of apologetics to save faith
from the disaster of religion, an artful deception de-

signed to regain from one hand what the other hand has been forced to yield. The distinction between religion and faith is not a gratuitous one; it must be carefully considered. In seeking to understand this distinction I will perhaps fall short of my aim. But I think that this is the unavoidable position of a philosopher confronted with the dialectic between religion, atheism, and faith. The philosopher is not a preacher. He may listen to the preachers, as I try to do, but he does not speak with their finality; his discourse is a preparatory discourse.

Being unable to cover here the whole range of questions suggested by "Religion, Atheism, and Faith," I shall concentrate on two topics—accusation and consolation. I choose these topics because they represent the two main functions of religion: taboo and shelter. And these two fundamental activities determine the two poles of religious feeling, at least in its crudest and most archaic form—the fear of punishment and the desire for protection. The same figure, the same image of the primitive god, both threatens and comforts primitive man. I take religion to be this archaic system, which faith must always overcome. Accusation and consolation are, so to speak, the rotten points of religion—in the same sense that Karl Marx used to call religion itself the rotten point of philosophy. In these "rotten points" atheism finds its raison d'être, a twofold role as destroyer and liberator. In destroying the shelter offered by religion and liberating men from the taboos imposed by religion, atheism clears the ground for a faith beyond accusation and consolation.

On Accusation

THE KIND OF ATHEISM which I have in mind in this inquiry is the atheism of Nietzsche and Freud. Why this choice? It is not enough to answer that they are the best exponents of the critique of religion as a cycle of prohibition, accusation, punishment, and condemnation; more important is the question of why they were able to attack religion in this way. They were able to do so because they created a new kind of hermeneutic, quite different from the critique of religion rooted in the tradition of British empiricism or of French positivism. They did not take the approach of disputing the so-called proofs of the existence of God; neither did they argue that the concept of God is meaningless. Instead they created a mode of critique in which cultural representations and creeds are considered as symptoms of disguised wishes and fears. For Nietzsche and Freud the cultural dimension of human existence, to which ethics and religion belong, has a hidden meaning which requires a specific mode of decipherment. Illusion, which keeps the true meaning of religion from the observer, is distinct from mere "error," in the epistemological sense of the word, and from "deception," in the moral sense. The illusions of our consciousness can be compared to a palimpsest, a text written over another text. Nietzsche and Freud developed parallel systems of reductive hermeneutics for revealing and clarifying the primary, underlying text. Their hermeneutics may be thought of as both a philology and a "genealogy." They are philological in that they are modes of exegesis or interpretation aimed at discovering the true text beneath the distortions of illusion. They are "genealogical" in attempting to trace the origin of the conflict between instincts and counterinstincts that results in the distortion of reality. The "genealogy" of illusion traced by Freud or Nietzsche is not concrete or strictly chronological, however. Even when it has recourse to historical stages, it points not to a true temporal origin but rather to a virtual, ideal focus, from which the values of ethics and religion proceed. To show that this focus is unreal and to reorient human values to a real focus, to their true origin, such is the task of the Freudian and Nietzschean hermeneutics. The fact that Nietzsche calls the real origin the will to power, while Freud calls it the libido, is incidental to the present argument. In spite of the differences of background, of concern, even of intention, between Freud and Nietzsche, their respective analyses of religion as a source of prohibition reinforce one another. We may even say that we understand each of them better when we view them together.

Nietzsche, on the one hand, shows that the so-called ideal is a "locus" outside and above the earthly will; it is an illusion of the slave will, which out of weakness projects itself into heaven. This illusory locus, described by traditional metaphysics as the intelligible, the absolute good, the transcendent and invisible origin of values, is the God of interdiction, from whom prohibition and condemnation flow. Because this ideal construction is an empty illusion, the destruction of metaphysics, which is occurring in our time, must take the form of nihilism. It is not Nietzsche who invented nihilism, neither nihilism which invented nothingness. Nihilism is a historical phenomenon to which Nietzsche is a witness; it is only the discovery of the nothingness inherent in the illusory origin of religious and ethical values. Nihilism is an expression of the very soul of metaphysics, since metaphysics postulates an ideal and supernatural origin and thereby exhibits nothing else than a contempt for life, a disparaging of the earth, a hatred of the instincts, and a resentment of the powerful by the weak. Christianity is affected by this reductive hermeneutics inasmuch as it is merely "a Platonism for the people," a variety of supernaturalism in ethics. Finally, Nietzsche's *Umwertung,* the "transvaluation," the reversal of values, is merely the reversal of a reversal, the reinstatement of the real origin of values, that is, the will to power.

This well-known critique of religion by Nietzsche, from *Beyond Good and Evil* and the *Genealogy of Morals,* is a good introduction to the hermeneutics of Freud. Psychoanalysis is in its own way both an exegesis and a "genealogy." It allows us to read the Oedipean drama behind the official text of consciousness, and it traces the energies invested in the process of repression to forces borrowed from the id, that is, from the depth of life itself. The superego, lifted above the ego, is a tribunal, an *Instanz*, which spies, judges, and condemns. Like the God of traditional metaphysics as analyzed by Nietzsche, the superego, seen by Freud as the source of condemnation and prohibition, is an ideal construction. The superego is thus neither primary nor absolute; it is a derived and dependent institution or elaboration. Of course there is an important aspect of Freud which is not common to Nietzsche: Freud's reduction of the ethical conscience to the superego was due to a convergence between his clinical experience with obsessional neurosis, such as melancholia and masochism, and his knowledge of the sociology of culture. From these two realms of experience Freud was able to elaborate what we might call a pathology of duty or of conscience. The genesis of neurosis in individuals gave him a key for understanding the genesis of totem and taboo in societies. These ethnological phenomena, which Freud saw as the earliest manifestations of our ethical and religious consciousness, appeared to be motivated by a hidden father image, related to the Oedipus complex observed in individuals. The individual Oedipus complex was used by Freud as a model for understanding this collective Oedipus complex which developed during the ancient history of mankind; the social institution of law was then linked by him to a primitive drama, the "murder of the father." It is difficult to say, however, whether this is only a myth of psychoanalysis, a Freudian myth, or whether Freud truly arrives at the origin of the gods. In any case, even if we have here only the personal mythology of Freud, it expresses an intuition very close to that of Nietzsche in the *Genealogy of Morals*. Both thinkers maintain that the belief in an absolute origin of good and evil originated in a situation of weakness and dependence. For Freud the *Umwertung*, the transvaluation—which I have described as a reversal of a prior reversal—involves not only the cultural ordeal which Nietzsche called nihilism but also a personal renunciation which Freud calls in his *Leonardo da Vinci* the "renunciation of the father." This renunciation can be compared to the process, or "work," of mourning, of which Freud speaks elsewhere. Nihilism and mourning, then, are the two parallel ways by which the true origin of values—that is, the will to power, or Eros in its eternal struggle against Thanatos—is regained.

Now if we wish to ascertain the theological significance of this kind of atheism, we should first further distinguish the character of this atheism. Everybody knows the famous saying "God is dead" from *Die fröhliche Wissenschaft*. But which god is dead? Who killed him (since his death is a murder)? And what kind of authority belongs to the word which proclaims his death? The answers to these three questions qualify the atheism of Nietzsche and Freud in contradistinction to the atheism of English empiricism or of French positivism, which is neither exegetical nor genealogical in the sense that I have stated.

Which god is dead? We may answer: the God of

metaphysics—and also of theology, inasmuch as theology relies on the metaphysics of a first cause, of a necessary being, of a prime mover which is absolute goodness and the origin of values. Let us say that it is the God of ontotheology, to use the word coined by Heidegger.

Ontotheology found its highest expression, at least with respect to ethics, in the Kantian philosophy. Kant links religion and ethics very closely: to consider the commandments of conscience as the commandments of God, such is the first function of religion. Of course religion has other functions according to Kant, in relation to the problem of evil, the realization of freedom, and the totalization of will and nature in an ethical world. But thanks to his initial link between God, as the supreme legislator, and the law of reason, Kant belongs to the age of metaphysics and remains faithful to the fundamental dichotomy it saw between the intelligible and the sensible world. The function of the Nietzschean and Freudian critiques is to submit the "principle of obligation," onto which is grafted Kant's concept of an ethical God, to a regressive analysis. Such an analysis deprives the principle of obligation of its a priori character. Reductive hermeneutics paves the way for a genealogy of the "a priori." It becomes evident that what seemed at first to be a prerequisite—that is to say, the formal principle of obligation—is in reality an act of accusation rooted in the will. This accusation cannot be discovered by a reflective philosophy such as Kant's, which separates a priori knowledge from empirical truths. Only a hermeneutical procedure is able to discover the accusation inherent in obligation. In substituting a philological and genealogical method for a merely abstractive method such as Kant's categorical analysis, reductive hermeneutics discovers behind the cold "practical reason" a function of the instincts, an expression of fear and desire. From beneath the apparent "autonomy of will" emerges the resentment of a particular will, the will of the weak. Thanks to this exegesis and genealogy, the moral God is revealed to be the God of accusation and condemnation —to use Nietzsche's terms. Such is the God that is dead.

Who is his murderer? As I have said before, not the atheist, but the very nothingness which dwells in the Ideal, the lack of absoluteness of the superego. The murder of the moral God is what Nietzsche described as a cultural process, the process of nihilism, and what Freud described in more psychological terms as the work of mourning applied to the father image.

When we turn to the third question—What kind of reliability has the word which proclaims the death of the moral God?—everything suddenly becomes problematic. We thought that we knew which God died—the moral God. We thought that we knew the cause of his death: the self-destruction of metaphysics through its implied nihilism. But everything becomes dubious as soon as we ask who says that. The "Madman" who lit a lantern in the bright morning hours and cried "I seek God"? Zarathustra? Perhaps the "Madman" as Zarathustra? At least we may say, in negative terms, that this is not a demonstrative way of thinking. Nietzsche, "the man with the hammer," has the authority only of the message which he proclaims, the sovereignty of the will to power. Nothing proves that his message is correct, except the kind of new life which it is able to inspire—only the Yea given to Dionysos, only love of fate, the acquiescence to the "eternal recurrence" of all things. But this positive aspect of the philosophy of Nietzsche, which alone could give authority to his negative hermeneutics, is itself trapped within the ruins which he pulled down around him. Perhaps no one is able to live at the level of Zarathustra. Certainly Nietzsche himself is not the superman he announces; his aggression against Christianity remains too full of resentment. The rebel is not, and cannot be, worth the prophet. The main work of Nietzsche after *Zarathustra* remains an accusation of accusation and falls short of the pure affirmation of life proclaimed by Zarathustra. This is why I think that nothing is decided and that all remains open after Nietzsche. Only one lane, it seems to me, is closed by Nietzsche—that of an ontotheology culminating in a moral God who would be the principle and foundation for an ethics of prohibition and condemnation. I think that we are henceforth unable to return to a form of moral life which would consist merely of submission to the commandments of a foreign or supreme will. We must acknowledge that the critique of ethics and religion by the "school of suspicion" has been an asset. From it we have learned to question the authority of a weak superego too easily identified with the will of God and to recognize that the commandment which gives death but not life is merely a projection of our own weakness.

As I ventured to suggest in my introductory remarks, atheism's significance is not limited to its destruction of the "moral God" and its refutation of the archaic, fear-inspired form of religion. Atheism opens a new path to faith, though a path full of uncertainties and dangers. We might be tempted not to follow this path but to leap instead directly to its destination. A philosopher, however, cannot go so far so quickly. Only a preacher, a prophetic preacher, would have the strength and the freedom of Nietzsche's Zarathustra and would be able both to return to the roots of Judeo-Christian faith and to make of this return an event appropriate to our time. This preaching would be at the same time primitive and postreligious because its return to the origins of faith would be a new beginning for our time. The philosopher is of course not such a prophetic preacher; at best he is, as Kierkegaard called himself, "the poet of the religious." This philosopher envisions a prophetic preacher who would actualize for our time this message of Exodus, which is prior to any law: "I am the Lord thy God, who brought thee out of the land of Egypt out of the house of bondage." He envisions a preacher who would pronounce only a word of liberation relevant to our time, and no word of prohibition or of condemnation; who would preach the Cross and the Resurrection of Christ as the beginning of a creative life and would define for our time all the consequences of the Paulinian antinomy between Gospel and Law. According to this antinomy, sin itself would be seen not as the transgression of prohibitions but as the antithesis of life under grace—that is, as life under law, the mode of human existence trapped in the infernal circle of law, transgression, guilt, and rebellion.

The contemporary philosopher in particular is not a prophetic preacher, for several reasons: First, he belongs to a time of desiccation and thirst in which Christianity as a cultural institution is truly "a Platonism for the people," a "law" in the Paulinian sense. Second, the process of nihilism has not reached its end, perhaps not even its peak; the work of mourning over the dead gods is not finished. The philosopher thinks in this intermediary time. The contemporary philosopher stands midway between atheism and faith; he cannot be satisfied with merely juxtaposing a reductive hermeneutic which enthrones the idols of the dead gods, and a positive hermeneutic which would be a recollection, a retrieve beyond the death of the moral God, of the biblical kerygma, that of the message of the prophets and of the primitive Christian community. It is the responsibility of the philosopher to delve into the character of the present antinomy until he finds the level of questioning which makes possible a mediation between religion and faith through atheism.

The path from atheism to faith must be circuitous. It may even appear to be, like the essays which Heidegger presents as *Holzwege*, a forest path which leads nowhere except to the forest itself and to the work of the woodcutter. I propose that as our first step along this difficult path we consider our relation to words—the word of the poet or the word of the thinker or any word which says

something about beings and Being. In the primary relation between an individual and any meaningful word is
implied a kind of obedience devoid of ethical tone. This
nonethical obedience delivers us from the theory of values, in which modern philosophy appears to be ensnared.
Indeed, I consider that modern philosophy is at a complete dead end on the problem of the origin of values; we
are condemned to oscillate between an impossible fabri-
cation of values and an impossible intuition of values.
Our failure to reconcile these two systems is reflected in
the antinomy of submission and rebellion which now infect pedagogy, politics, and everyday ethics. We must retreat from this dead end and try a nonethical approach
to the problem of autonomy and obedience; the only
way to think ethically is first to think nonethically.

To think nonethically, we must start at a point where
the autonomy of our will is rooted in a dependence and
an obedience which are not infected by accusation, prohibition, and condemnation. Listening is just such a preethical situation. It is a mode of being which is not yet a
mode of doing, and for this reason it escapes the alternatives of submission and revolt. Heraclitus used to say
"Do not hear my words but the Logos." When a word
says something, when it discloses not only something of
beings but of Being—as is the case with the word of the
poet or the thinker—we are confronted with what could
be called a "word-event," a word process. Something is
said of which I am not the origin, nor the owner. The
word—unlike the tools of work and production, or goods
to be consumed—is not at my disposal. In a word-event,

I dispose of nothing, I do not impose myself. I am no longer the master. I am led beyond care and concern. In this situation of nonmastery lies the origin of both obedience and freedom, as the following passage from Heidegger's *Being and Time* demonstrates:

We can make clear the connection of discourse with understanding and intelligibility by considering an existential possibility which belongs to talking itself—hearing. If we have not heard "aright," it is not by accident that we say we have not "understood." Hearing is constitutive for discourse. And just as linguistic utterance is based on discourse, so is acoustic perception on hearing. Listening to . . . is Dasein's existential way of Being-open as Being-with for Others. Indeed, hearing constitutes the primary and authentic way in which Dasein is open for its ownmost potentiality-for-Being—as in hearing the voice of the friend whom every Dasein carries with it. Dasein hears, because it understands. As a Being-in-the-world with Others, a Being which understands, Dasein is "in thrall" to Dasein-with and to itself; and in this thraldom it "belongs" to these. Being-with develops in listening to one another [*Aufeinander-hören*], which can be done in several possible ways: following, going along with, and the privative modes of not-hearing, resisting, defying, and turning away. [*Being and Time*, tr. from the German *Sein und Zeit* by John Macquarrie and Edward Robinson (New York, Harper & Row, 1962), pp. 206-7.]

It is not by mere chance that in many of the Western European languages the words for "obedience" are derived from the words for "hearing" or "listening." In Latin, for example, *obedientia* [obedience] is related to *obaudire* [to give ear to, to listen]. Similarly, in German "hearkening" is *horchen*, and the possibility of "obedience" (*gehorchen*) abides there. Words, hearkening, and obedience, therefore, are linked. To quote again from Heidegger:

It is on the basis of this potentiality for hearing, which is existentially primary, that anything like hearkening [*Horchen*] becomes possible. Hearkening is phenomenally still more primordial than what is defined "in the first instance" as "hearing" in psychology—the sensing of tones and the perception of sounds. Hearkening too has the kind of Being of the hearing which understands. (*Ibid.,* p. 207.)

The "hearing which understands," such is the knot of our problem. Of course, nothing has yet been said about the word as Word of God. The philosopher is still far from being able to point toward a word which would truly deserve to be called the Word of God, although he may designate the mode of being which makes the Word of God existentially possible—as we have read: "It is on the basis of this potentiality for hearing, which is existentially primary, that anything like hearkening [*Horchen*] becomes possible." Here for the first time, prior to any moral teaching, we recognize hearing as the basis for some other modes of heeding, or obeying, one another—for example, following (*folgen*) and the negative mode, nonheeding (*nicht-hören*). "Hearing" (*hören*), moreover, as the German words suggest, evokes "belonging" (*zugehören*); this is the preethical obedience to which I alluded earlier.

Not only is hearing existentially prior to obeying, but keeping silent precedes speaking. To keep silent is not the same as to be dumb, however. To keep silent is to let things be said by others. Silence opens a space for hearing:

Keeping silent is another essential possibility of discourse, and it has the same existential foundation. In talking with one another, the person who keeps silent can "make one understand" (that is, he can develop an understanding), and he can do so more authentically than the person who is never short of words. Speaking at length [*Viel-sprechen*] about something does not offer the slightest guarantee that thereby understanding is advanced. On the contrary, talking extensively about something, covers it up and brings what is understood to a sham clarity—the unintelligibility of the trivial. But to keep silent does not mean to be dumb. On the contrary, if a man is dumb, he still has a tendency to "speak." Such a person has not proved that he can keep silence; indeed, he entirely lacks the possibility of proving anything of the sort. And the person who is accustomed by Nature to speak little is no better able to show that he is keeping silent or that he is the sort of person who can do so. He who never says anything cannot keep silent at any given moment. Keeping silent authentically is possible only in genuine discoursing. To be able to keep silent, Dasein must have something to say—that is, it must have at its disposal an authentic and rich disclosedness of itself. In that case one's reticence [*Verschwiegenheit*] makes something manifest, and does away with "idle talk" ["*Gerede*"]. As a mode of discoursing, reticence Articulates the intelligibility of Dasein in so primordial a manner that it gives rise to a potentiality-for-hearing which is genuine, and to a Being-with-one-another which is transparent. (*Ibid.*, p. 208.)

Silence is the origin of hearing and of obedience.

Heidegger's analysis of "hearing" and its relation to *Dasein* prepares the way for understanding a human relation to God as Word which is prior to prohibition and accusation. We will not arrive at the word-event which calls itself the Gospel through a mere extension of the categories of Heidegger's analysis, however. The God whom we seek is not the source of moral obligation, the author of commandments, the one who could put the seal of the Absolute on the ethical experience of man. On the contrary, this inquiry convinces me that the kerygma must not be caught in the snare of obligation and duty.

And now the second step on our circuitous path toward faith: What kind of ethic can be based on an existential relation to the Word? We must keep in mind that atheism has destroyed the moral God and that hearing and keeping silent involve a nonethical mode of understanding. We will then be prepared to formulate the new ethic in terms which do not imply—at least in the beginning—prohibition, terms which are still neutral with respect to accusation and condemnation. Let us therefore elaborate the original ethical problem, toward which point both the destruction of the moral God and the nonethical instruction by the Word.

I shall call this ethic prior to the ethic of obligation an ethic of the desire to be or of the effort to exist. The history of philosophy offers us here an invaluable precedent, the thought of Spinoza. Spinoza defines Ethics as the entire process by which man passes from bondage to beatitude and freedom. This process is ruled not by a formal principle of obligation, still less by an intuition of ends and values, but by the unfolding of the effort or "conatus" which posits each of us as a finite mode of being. I have said "effort," but I must also say "desire," because at the core of this ethic is the identity between effort, in the sense of the "conatus" of Spinoza and desire, in the sense of the "Eros" of Plato and Freud (Freud does not hesitate to say that what he calls libido and Eros is akin to the Eros of the *Symposium*). By "effort" I mean the affirmative power of existing, which is articulated in the most fundamental expression of affirmation: I am, *ich bin, je suis*. This affirmative power has been alienated in many ways, however (therein lies the problem of evil). It must be recaptured, regained. To reappropriate our effort to exist is in fact the task of ethics. Because our power to be has been alienated, the effort to exist remains a desire; "desire" here as everywhere implies a lack or a need. This lack at the very center of our existence makes of our effort a desire and equates the "conatus" of Spinoza with the "Eros" of Plato and Freud. The affirmation of being in the lack of being, such is the essence of an existential ethics. Ethics in this fundamental sense, then, is the progressive reappropriation of our effort to be.

The fundamental character of ethics is obscured if obligation is considered the main principle of practical reason. The formalism of the ethics of obligation obscures the dialect of human action, or, to use a stronger phrase,

the dialectic of the human act of existing. This dialectic
is revealed by the problems inherent in assuming an a
priori basis for practical reason. Kant borrowed his notion of an a priori foundation for practical reason, it
seems to me, from his earlier work, the *Critique of Pure
Reason*. There it is perfectly relevant to his regressive
analysis of the categorical structures which make possible an act of knowledge. But I doubt whether the same
dichotomy between the empirical and the a priori is also
relevant to the inner structure of human action, to what
I have called the dialectic of the act of existing. Kant's
transfer of that dichotomy to his notion of practical reason is responsible for his opposition of obligation, considered by him as the a priori of the will, and desire,
which for him represents the empirical element of action. The exclusion of desire from the ethical sphere has
tremendous consequences: the search for happiness is no
longer regarded as a principle of the will by the moralist;
the formal principle of obligation is thus isolated from
the process of action, and an ethical rigorism replaces
the Spinozistic conception of beatitude and freedom. It
seems to me that the hermeneutics of Nietzsche and
Freud undermine this notion of a formalist foundation
of ethics. Ethical formalism is seen to be a second-rate
rationalization based on a transfer of transcendental-
empirical distinctions to the realm of practical reason
from the realm of theoretical reason.

I do not mean to say that the principle of obligation
has no ethical pertinence. Even prohibition has its place;
but it is not an origin, not a principle. At best it is an

objective criterion by which to judge our intentions. The same thing could be said of the concept of value; it also has a place, but not a primary one. The notion of value arises at the stage of ethical theorizing when we must determine our power to be according to the situation, the institutions, the structure of economic, political, and cultural life. The notion of value appears at the intersection of our indefinite desire to be and the finite conditions of its actualization. This function of value scarcely allows me to hypostatize *the* Value, still less to adore the idols of Value. It is enough to relate value and the process of evaluation to the dialectics of action and to the history of human ethical experience.

Not only the hermeneutics of Nietzsche and Freud invite us to refer ethical formalism and the process of value-formation to the existential basis of our effort and desire to be. The kind of philosophy of the word which we developed earlier also invites us to do so. When we speak of the word as a living and effective word, we evoke a connection between the word and the active core of our existence. We imply that the word has the power to change the understanding we have of ourselves. Its power is not primarily imperative in nature, however. Before the word addresses itself to our will as an order and elicits obedience, it addresses itself to what I called our existence and elicits effort and desire; it changes us, not because a will is imposed on our will but because of the effort made by "the hearing which understands." The word reaches us at the level of the symbolic structures of our existence, the dynamic schemes which express our way of understanding our situation and of projecting our power in that situation. Our existence as capable of being modified by the word is prior to the will, therefore, and even prior to the principle of obligation, which according to Kant is the a priori principle of the will. The inner connection between our desire to be and the power of the word is a consequence of the act of listening, of hearkening, which I discussed earlier. This connection in its turn makes possible will, evaluation, decision, choice. These phenomena are only the surface projections of the underlying relationship between our sense of situation, our understanding, and our discourse, to refer again to the main notions in Heidegger's analysis of *Dasein*.

On Consolation

THE CONNECTION
between accusation and consolation is perhaps the most
striking feature of religion. God threatens and protects.
He is the ultimate danger and the ultimate shield. In the
most rudimentary theologies, of which we find remnants
in the Old Testament, the two sides of the deity are rationally reconciled in the law of retribution. The God
who threatens and also protects is a moral God. By ulti-
mately rewarding righteousness with bliss and wicked-
ness with suffering, he corrects the apparent disorder in
the distribution of human fortune. The law of retribution makes of religion not only an absolute foundation
for moral law but also a world view, a speculative cosmology. As Providence (*pronoia* in Greek, *providentia* in
Latin) the moral God is the ruler of a world which obeys
the law of retribution. That law characterizes perhaps
the most archaic and most widespread of all religious
world views. But it does not exhaust all the possible relations of man to God, and there have always been men
of faith who discarded it as wholly impious. Already in
the Babylonian and biblical literature known as wisdom

literature, and above all in the Book of Job, unadulterated faith in God is opposed with great force to faith motivated by the law of retribution and is described as a tragic faith beyond any assurance or protection.

Atheism must mean the destruction of the moral God not only as the ultimate source of accusation but as the ultimate source of protection, as Providence. But if atheism is to have any religious significance, the death of the providential God should point toward a new faith, a tragic faith which would be to classical metaphysics what the faith of Job was to the archaic law of retribution professed by his pious friends. By "metaphysics" I mean here the intricate fabric of philosophy and theology which culminates in theodicy, the defense or vindication of God's goodness and omnipotence in view of the existence of evil. Leibniz's theodicy is the paradigm of all attempts to understand the order of this world as providential; that is, as expressing the subordination of physical laws to ethical laws established by a righteous God.

I do not intend to criticize theodicy on epistemological grounds, as Kant did in his famous essays against the Leibnizian and post-Leibnizian theodicies. I prefer to consider instead, in conformity with the preceding chapter, the atheistic contentions of Freud and Nietzsche, whose critique of the moral God finds its full realization in the argument against religion as refuge and protection. The critique developed by Freud and Nietzsche goes further than an epistemological critique; probing beyond the level of formal logic and methods of argument, it reveals the underlying motivations of theodicy. The substitution of hermeneutics for epistemology bears not only on theodicy, as exemplified by Leibniz, but on all philosophies which claim to overcome theodicy and yet resort to a rational reconciliation between opposing forces in nature and human reality. Thus, though criticizing Leibniz, Kant attempts, with his postulates of practical reason, to reconcile freedom and nature under the rule of the moral God. Likewise, Hegel in turn criticizes Kant and his moral world view, yet builds a rational system in which all contradictions are reconciled. In Hegel's system, the ideal is no longer opposed to the real; the ideal, the intelligible, is considered the law of the real. Hegel's philosophy appears to Nietzsche to be essentially a moral philosophy. Of course, Nietzsche's violent reduction of philosophies as different as those of Leibniz, Kant, and Hegel—all of which he considers to be primarily moral in character—cannot be accepted by the historian of philosophy, who must protect the singular rational structure of each of these philosophies against such a confusion. Nietzsche, however, by first reducing and negating the evident differences between the great philosophies of the past, is able to arrive at a common motive behind even the most diverse philosophies. He shows that common to Leibniz's theodicy, Kant's postulates of practical reason, and Hegel's concept of absolute knowledge is a search for rational reconciliation. For Nietzsche, the will which hides behind these rationalistic systems is always a weak will; its weakness consists precisely in its recourse to a world view whose ethical principle, which Nietzsche calls the Ideal, dominates the process of reality. The value of this critique is, therefore, to transform the epistemological critique of teleology into a hermeneutic of the will to power, and to refer the philosophical doctrines of the past to the degree of weakness or strength of the will, to its negative or positive disposition, its reactive or active impulsion.

In the preceding chapter, we interrupted the Nietzschean hermeneutic at the point where it is an "accusation of accusation." It was appropriate to stop at that point in a discussion devoted to prohibition. Furthermore, Nietzsche's own approach encourages us to emphasize the critical side of this work: for the most part this work does constitute an accusation of accusation and seems to flow from the kind of resentment that he reproaches in the moralist.

In this chapter we must go further, however. Our critique of metaphysics and of its search for rational reconciliation must arrive at a positive ontology beyond resentment and accusation. Such a positive ontology lies in a completely nonethical view, which Nietzsche describes as "the innocence of becoming" (*die Unschuld des Werdens*), or "beyond good and evil." This kind of ontology cannot be made dogmatic unless it is subjected to its own critique; and perhaps it will not escape self-destruction in the process. Moreover, such an ontology is inevitably entangled in some form of mythology—either mythology in the Greek sense of the word, such as the mythology of Dionysos; or mythology in the sense of modern cosmology, such as the myth of the eternal recurrence of all things, with its "love of fate"; or mythology in the sense of the philosophy of history, such as the myth of the superman; or, finally, a mythology beyond the opposition between these three, such as the myth of the world as play or as a game. All these mythologies say the same thing: they proclaim the guiltlessness, the non-ethical character, of the whole of being.

The kind of mythology represented by Nietzsche's idea of the "guiltlessness of becoming" has a prosaic counterpart in what Freud called "the principle of reality." It is not by chance that Freud sometimes gives this principle another name, "Ananke" (meaning the ultimate fate, to which all beings must yield), which is borrowed from the tradition of Greek tragedy and recalls "the love of fate" in Nietzsche. Of course Freud always opposed the principle of reality to the principle of pleasure and to all ways of thinking which are influenced by the principle of pleasure, among them the delusive way of thinking which we call wishful thinking.

It is in relation to the principle of pleasure that a second critique of religion occurs in Freud's work. Fundamentally, religion for him is not just an absolute sanction given to the requirements of conscience, let us say in Freudian terms, of the superego; it is a compensation for the hardness of life. Religion in that sense has the highest function of culture; its task is to protect man against the superiority of nature and to compensate him for the sacrifices of instinct required by life in society. According to this interpretation the aspect that religion presents to the individual is one of protection rather than prohibition. It appeals to desire rather than to fear.

This reductive, regressive analysis of the protective aspect of religion brings us back to the notion of a collective father image, just as the analysis of prohibition did. But the father figure is now ambiguous, ambivalent: it protects as well as reproaches; it is inspired not only by our fear of punishment but by our desire for protection and consolation. This desire is in essence a longing for the father. Thus religion as Freud sees it is an expression of the pleasure principle in one of its most intricate and disguised modes. The principle of reality must therefore involve a renunciation of the longing for the father at the level of our desires as well as at the level of our fears. A world view deprived of the father image is the price to pay for this *ascesis* of desire.

At this point Freud overtakes Nietzsche: Freud's substitution of the principle of reality for the principle of pleasure has the same meaning as Nietzsche's substitution of the concept of the innocence of becoming and the notion of the world as play, or as a game, for a moral world view. Freud's tone is less lyrical than Nietzsche's; it is closer to resignation than to jubilation. Freud knew too much of the distress of man to venture beyond a mere acceptance of the inexorable order of nature, and he was too dependent on a coldly scientific world view to give way to unrestrained lyricism. Nevertheless, in his last works, the theme of Ananke is softened and balanced by another theme, which brings him closer to Nietzsche—I refer to the theme of Eros, which brings Freud back to the Faustian motive of his youth, previously overshadowed by his scientific preoccupations. The philosophical mood of Freud is perhaps determined by the outcome of the struggle within his personality between a positivistic sense of reality and a romantic sense of life. When the romantic sense takes hold, we hear a voice which could be that of Nietzsche: "And now we may expect that the other of the two heavenly powers, the eternal Eros, will affirm itself in its struggle against its no less immortal adversary"—the adversary being Thanatos, death. The idea that a great drama between Eros and Thanatos underlies the inexorable order of nature is the echo of Nietzsche in Freud. Of course Freud's discreet mythology has neither the lyrical nor the philosophical power of Nietzsche's mythology, but it makes Nietzsche more accessible to us. Through Freud something comes to us of the difficult teaching set down by Nietzsche at Sils-Maria.

What kind of faith deserves to survive the critique of Freud and Nietzsche? In my first chapter I spoke of a kind of prophetic preaching which would return to the origins of Judeo-Christian faith and yet be an appropriate beginning for our time. In relation to the problem of accusation that preaching would pronounce only a word of liberation and would make clear all the consequences for our time of the Paulinian antinomy between Gospel and Law. In relation to the problem of consolation, that prophetic preaching would be heir to the tragic faith of Job. It would adopt the same attitude toward the teleological metaphysics of Western philosophy that Job did toward the pious discourses of his friends about the God of retribution. It would be a faith that wanders in the darkness, in a "new night of the understanding"—to use the language of the mystics—before a God who has not the attributes of "Providence." This God does not protect me but delivers me up to the dangers of a life worthy of being called human. Is not this God the Crucified, the dying God, the God whose weakness alone may help me? The new night of the understanding is a night for our desire as much as for our fear, a night for our longing for a protective father. Beyond this night, and only beyond it, will be recovered the true meaning of the God of consolation, the God of the Resurrection, the Pantocrator of Byzantine and Romanesque imagery.

Though I can envision the prophetic preacher and sometimes imagine his words, I cannot perform his function. The philosopher's method is not to reconcile in a weak eclecticism the hermeneutic which destroys the old idols with the hermeneutic which retrieves the kerygma. Instead, the philosophical progression from religion to faith through atheism involves a purification of man's desire for protection and a purification of man's fear of punishment—inseparable processes, both of which are beyond what Nietzsche called "the spirit of revenge."

We have found in our relation to the Word the starting point, the origin and model of an "obedience to Being" beyond any fear of punishment, beyond prohibition and condemnation. Perhaps we may discover in that very obedience the source of a consolation which would be as far beyond the childish desire for protection as obedience itself is far from any fear of punishment. My initial relation to the Word, when I receive it as wholly meaningful, not only neutralizes all accusation and, by that means, all fear, but excludes my desire for protection; it parenthesizes, so to speak, the narcissism of my desire. I enter a realm of meaning where the question is not of myself but of Being as such. The whole of Being is made manifest in the oblivion of my desires and interests.

The display of Being in the absence of personal concern was already implied in the revelation which ends the Book of Job: "Then the Lord answered Job out of a whirlwind and said"—but what did He say? Nothing which could be considered an answer to the problem of human suffering and death, nothing which could be used as a theodicy, as a justification of God; on the contrary, what is spoken is of an order alien to man, of a measure which has no proportion to man: "Where wast thou when I laid the foundations of the earth? Tell me if thou hast understanding," says the Lord. The way to a theodicy is closed. Even the vision of the behemoth and the leviathan which culminates the revelation has no connection with the personal problem of Job. No teleology issues from the whirlwind, no intelligible connection between a physical and an ethical order. There is only the display of the whole of Being in the fullness of the Word. There remains only the possibility of acceptance, of resignation, which is the first stage of a consolation beyond the desire for protection.

Why does resignation to a nonethical order of the whole of Being constitute the first stage of consolation?

Because, although a nonethical order is alien to my narcissistic interests, it is not alien to discourse. Being may be brought into words.

For Job the revelation of the whole is first not a sight but a voice. The Lord speaks; that is the essential. He does not speak of Job; He speaks to Job, and that is sufficient. The word-event as such creates a link; the dialogue situation is itself a mode of consolation. The word-event is a word-becoming of Being. The hearing of the Word makes possible the sight of the world as order: "With the hearing of the ear, I have heard thee, but now my eye sees thee." Even now Job's question about himself is not solved but dissolved by the shift of center which the Word effects.

Here our attention is directed away from Job to the pre-Socratics. The pre-Socratic thinkers also perceived the shift of center effected by the Word. "To be and to be thought are one and the same." Therein is the fundamental possibility for consolation. The unity of Being and Logos makes it possible for man to belong to the whole as a speaking being. Because my word belongs to the Word, because the speaking of my language belongs to the saying of Being, I do not need to reconcile my desires with the order of nature. In this kind of belonging is the origin not only of obedience beyond fear but of consent beyond desire.

Let us elaborate this concept of "consent"—but not in psychological terms. A philosopher, unlike a therapist, cures desires by changing ideas. Therefore, to go from a longing for protection to a consent to the whole of Being he must take the difficult approach of examining the metaphysical system based on man's desire for protection.

The metaphysics in question here tries to bind values and facts within a unifying system, which we like to call the sense of the universe or the sense of life. In such a system the natural order and the ethical order are unified within the framework of a higher order of totality. But Heidegger suggests that perhaps this attempt comes about precisely because we have forgotten the unity which the pre-Socratics recognized when they spoke of the sameness of Being and Logos. The very concepts "value" and "fact," between which we divide the realm of reality, imply the loss of primordial unity, in which there are not yet values and facts, neither ethics nor physics. We must not be surprised then if we are unable to consolidate the fragments left by the loss of the principle of unity. For my part I think this point of Heidegger's is well taken. It may be that the whole reasoning of classical metaphysics on the subordination of causal laws to final laws represents a desperate attempt to recreate a unity in place of the fundamental unity of Being, which has been forgotten. In an essay called "The Age of the World-View" Heidegger characterizes the age of metaphysics as that age in which "the existent" (*die Seiende*) is "put at the disposal of available 'representation' (*Vorstellung*). . . . In the metaphysics of Descartes that the existent was defined for the first time as objectivity of representation, and truth as certainty of representation" (tr. Marjorie Grene, *Measure*, II [1951], 277). Now the world becomes a *Bild,* a picture: "Where the world becomes a view, the existent as a whole is posited as that with respect to which a man orients himself, which therefore he wishes to bring and have before himself and thus in a decisive sense re-present to himself" (*Ibid.,* p. 279). At the same time the representational character of the existent is the correlate of the emergence of man as subject. Man pushes himself to the center of the picture. Henceforth the existent is brought before man as what is objective and may be disposed of. Later—with Kant, with Fichte, and finally with Nietzsche himself—man as subject becomes man as will. Will appears as the origin of values, whereas the world as picture recedes to the background as mere fact, with no value. Nihilism is not far off. The gap can no longer be bridged between a subject which posits itself as the origin of values and a world which displays itself as a set of appearances deprived of value. As long as we continue to regard the world as an object for representation and the human will as the positor of values, conciliation and integration are impossible. Nihilism is the historical verification of this impossibility. In particular, nihilism lays bare the failure of the metaphysical God to bring about this reconciliation— the failure of all attempts to supplement causality with teleology.

We have to reason back to a state earlier than this subject-object dichotomy if we want to overcome the antinomies which proceed from it, the antinomy between value and fact, between teleology and causality, between man and world. But this regression does not lead us back into the indeterminate darkness of a philosophy of identity; it leads us into the disclosure of Being as the Logos which gathers together all things.

If we are right, the beginning of an answer to Nietzsche lies in a meditation on the Logos which gathers together all things, rather than in an emergence of the will to power, which perhaps still belongs to the age of metaphysics (in which man was defined as will). For Heidegger the Logos is the aspect or dimension of our language connected to the question of Being; by means of the Logos the question of Being is put into words. Thanks to the Logos man emerges not only as a will to power but as a being which inquires on Being.

If man is fundamentally posited as man only when he is gathered in by the Logos which "gathers together" all things, consolation is possible for him in the bliss of belonging to the Logos and to Being as Logos. This bliss occurs first in poetizing (*Urdichtung*); secondly in thinking. Heidegger says somewhere that a poet sees the Holy, and a thinker sees Being. They stand on different mountains, but their voices echo one another.

There are other ways in which Heidegger alludes to the function of the Logos as consolation. He says, for example, that the Logos of the pre-Socratics is the same as Physis. It is not nature, as opposed to convention or to history or to the spiritual. It is something which by gathering dominates. It is "the Overpowering" (*das überwaltigende*). Once more we are reminded of the connection between Job and the pre-Socratics. There was already in the revelation of the Book of Job an experience

of the Overpowering and an experience of being joined
to the Overpowering. This happens neither physically
nor spiritually nor mystically, but merely in the clarity of
"saying" (*Sagen*). Not only does "Logos" mean the
power which makes manifest and which gathers together, but it associates the poet with this gathering together under the overpowering of Physis. The power of
gathering things together through language does not belong primarily to us as speaking subjects; gathering and
revelation belong first to the Overpowering symbolized
by the Physis of the early Greeks. Language is less and
less a work of man. The power to speak is not at our disposal, we are at its disposal; and it is because we are not
masters of our speaking that we may be "gathered in,"
that is to say, joined to what gathers. In this light our
language becomes something more than a practical
means of communication with others and of mastering
things; when speaking becomes "saying," or better, when
"saying" abides in the speaking of our language, then we
have the experience of language as a gift and of thought
as the recognition of this gift. Thought gives thanks for
the gift of language, and this is once more a form of consolation. Man is consoled when in language he lets
things be, or be shown. Because Job hears the Word as
gathering together he sees the world as gathered together: "With the hearing of the ear, I have heard thee,
but now my eye sees thee."

Kierkegaard calls this consolation "repetition." In the
Book of Job he sees this "repetition" expressed in myth-
ical form as a restitution: "And the Lord gave Job twice

as much as he had before." But if Kierkegaard's "repetition" is not just a different term for the law of retribution, which Job rejected, and a tardy justification of Job's
pious friends, whom the Lord condemned, it must mean
the consummation of hearing in seeing. This concept of
"repetition" can thus be identified with the terms of the
pre-Socratics; it is essentially the same as the pre-Socratic
understanding of "Logos" as a gathering together and of
"Physis" as an overpowering. Once more the Book of Job
and the fragments of Heraclitus say one and the same
thing.

In order to understand this last point let us return to
Nietzsche. Nietzsche, too, gave the name of "consolation" (*Trost*) to the great longing, "the greatest hope,"
that man be overcome. Why did he call this hope a consolation? Because it involves the deliverance from revenge (*Rache*): "That man be delivered from revenge,
there I find the bridge toward the highest hope and a
rainbow after long disturbances." The deliverance from
revenge is the heart of our meditation on consolation,
since revenge means that "where there was suffering,
there was to be punishment." Heidegger comments that
revenge is a pursuit which opposes itself and degrades—
not primarily in a moral sense, however. Nor is the critique of revenge a moral critique. The spirit of revenge is
directed against time and its passing. Zarathustra says:
"This, yea, this only is Revenge itself, the resentment of
the will against time and its 'there was.' " Revenge is the
"counterwill of will" (*des Willens Widerwille*) and it is
primarily a resentment against time. Time passing is the

adverse thing which makes the will suffer, and revenge degrades what passes as passing. To overcome revenge is to overcome the No in the Yea.

Is not the "recapitulation" of Zarathustra close to the "repetition" which Kierkegaard reads in the Book of Job and to the "gathering" which Heidegger reads in the pre-Socratics? The kinship cannot be denied; but the similarity would be even greater if Nietzsche's work itself did not belong to the spirit of revenge in that it is an accusation of accusation. In the last lines of *Ecce Homo* we read: "Have I been misunderstood? Dionysos against the Crucified." Therein lies the limitation of Nietzsche. And why is he unequal to the call of Zarathustra for overcoming revenge? Is it not because for Nietzsche the creation of the superman who can overcome revenge depends on the individual will and not on the Word, on discourse? Does not Nietzsche's "will to power" therefore remain both acceptance and revenge? Only the kind of *Gelassenheit* [release] which belongs to the submission of individual language to discourse is beyond revenge. Consent must be linked to poetry. Heidegger comments on the poem of Hölderlin which contains this verse: *dichterisch wohnt der Mensch* [in poetic fashion dwelleth man upon the earth]. Since poetizing begins to overcome the estrangement between man and world, through "building," it is the fundamental trait of human existence. It enables man to dwell upon the earth. Genuine dwelling occurs where there are poets. When man's relation to language is reversed, when language speaks, then man "answers" language by hearing what it says to him, and dwelling becomes "poetical." "Dwelling" is another name for the "repetition" of Kierkegaard. Dwelling is not flight from reality. In fact, Hölderlin says: "Full of merits, but in poetic fashion dwelleth man upon the earth." The poem suggests that man dwells on this earth to the extent that a tension is maintained between his concern for the heavens, for the divine, and the rooting of his existence in earth. This tension gives measure and assigns a place to the act of dwelling. In its most inclusive sense, "poetry" is that which roots the act of dwelling between heaven and earth, under heaven and on earth, in the power of the Word, of discourse, of saying. "Poetry" so defined is more than the making of poems; it is *poiesis,* the act of creation in the broadest sense.

In this philosophical inquiry into the religious significance of atheism, we have progressed from resignation to consent and from consent to a mode of dwelling on earth ruled by poetry and by thought. This mode of being is no longer "love of fate" but a love of creation, which accomplishes something of the movement from atheism to faith. Love of creation is a form of consolation that does not depend on external reward, and it is equally beyond revenge. Love finds in itself its reward; it is itself the consolation.

There is, I suggest, a certain congruence between this philosophical analysis and an interpretation of the kerygma which would be both faithful to the origins of Judeo-Christian faith and appropriate to our time. Biblical faith represents God—the God of the prophets and the God of the Christian Trinity—as a Father. Atheism teaches us to renounce this father image. Overcome as an idol, the father image may be recovered as a symbol, however. As a symbol it would be a parable of the ground of love; it would be the counterpart, in a theology of love, of the progression which led us from a mere resignation to Fate to a poetic life. Such, I believe, is the religious significance of atheism. An idol must die, in order that a symbol of Being may speak.